*Dear
Shadows*

Dear Shadows

PORTRAITS FROM MEMORY

John Wain

JOHN MURRAY
1986

© This collection, John Wain 1986

First published 1986
by John Murray (Publishers) Ltd
50 Albemarle Street, London W1X 4BD

Typeset by Inforum Ltd, Portsmouth
Printed and bound in Great Britain
by The Bath Press, Avon

British Library CIP data
Wain, John
Dear shadows: portraits from memory.
1. Biography—20th century
I. Title
920'.009'04   CT120
ISBN 0–7195–4284–7

Contents

ACKNOWLEDGEMENT

Some of these memoirs have been published separately:
'Julia' in *The American Scholar*; 'Nevill Coghill' in
Descant (Toronto) and, in shortened form, in *The Times
Educational Supplement*; 'Arnold' and 'The Incidental
Thoughts of Marshall McLuhan' in *Encounter*; 'Werner'
in *The London Magazine*. My thanks to those editors for
permission to reprint.

Foreword

T HIS BOOK started from a very simple impulse, and now that it is finished at last I do not think it has, except here and there, wandered far from that simplicity. My original wish was simply to bring to life on the page a number of people who were important to me at various times in my life and are now dead. Some of them were known to the wider world, others entirely unknown to it; but in either case I saw them, and think back on them, as private individuals; their effect on me was personal.

When I use the deliberately neutral and colourless expression 'they were important to me', I mean that I loved them and therefore, of course, that I still love them. People who cheat and rob us, who find pleasure in tormenting and humiliating us, leave our minds full of resentment and darkness. People who deal with us fairly, who treat us with kindness and generosity and share with us the resources of their lives, leave our minds full of contentment and light. Only the latter are worth writing about, for 'what will survive of us is love.'

One of the hardest sayings of Jesus (a prophet much given to hard sayings, to paradoxes, riddles, and those sullen dynamic metaphors which act like a concentrated elixir of poetry) is 'Let the dead bury their dead'. What would it be, I ask, for the dead to bury their dead? Would it be for the living to turn their backs entirely on everything that has gone before the brief sunlight of their own day? Surely not, for the prophet was too deep, and too addicted to irony, to mean anything so simple and single.

And if the dead are to bury their dead, what are they to bury them *in*? The earth? But the earth is full of memories; indeed, the soil is an emblem of time, being made up of dust-grains milled from rocks that witnessed the Creation, fragments of dead root that once nourished green shoots and stems, and, scattered through it all, seeds that carry within their tiny capsules the thrust of the future. What is it to be buried, thrust down out of sight, in this rich ferment? What is it to partake in the earth?

If I bury those dead friends about whom I write in this book, it is with that kind of burial, the launching into a new sphere of life, My title comes from Yeats's poem, 'In Memory of Eva Gore-Booth and Con Markievicz': that is to say, from an elegy on two sisters who have transcended the limitations of their dogma-ridden lives and indeed of all temporal life:

> Dear shadows, now you know it all.

I have written these essays in portraiture over the last five years, working entirely at my own pace and my own sweet will. When I wrote about someone it was always because that person had come and stood beside my chair and said 'Write about me'. Most of the essays were printed as soon as they were written, but on the other hand I always knew that what I was writing was a book, and it is a short book because I only wrote about people for the reason I have given, because they told me to; I was not at all tempted to think, when I had done half-a-dozen, that it would be a good thing to add a few more to bring the collection up to a decent size. The boat moved off not when it was full, but when all the passengers had shown the only kind of ticket I was accepting as valid.

This is a book, then, about other people. But, since the perceiving eye modifies the object, any book above the level of a collection of statistical tables or wiring diagrams is to some extent a book about the author. I met the individuals who compose this gallery of characters at different times of my life, and under different circumstances. To explain how each one affected me has necessarily involved a certain amount of explanation as to what point I had reached in my own journey, what needs in my own nature were satisfied by what I was able to give to, and receive from, each one. In *Sprightly Running*

(1962) I made a narrative of my own life up to the age of thirty-five; and sometimes, through the years, people have asked me if I intend to publish a sequel. I suppose, in a way, this is it.

J.W.
Summer 1985

Nevill Coghill

H E WAS A BIG MAN, with a tallness that would not be remarkable now that so many people are tall, but also built on generous lines, broad-shouldered and deep-chested. His head was large, and brown hair, greying in middle life, curled and clustered on it as wiry as heather. He smiled easily, revealing somewhat battered teeth, and indeed his whole face had a slightly rough, knocked-about quality, like a chipped statue. I had one friend who used to say that he looked like one of the emperors' heads outside the Sheldonian – the old pre-1970 ones, that had weathered badly. Another used to call him Neanderthal Man. But if his head was statue-like, it was a noble statue, generous in expression and bearing. His voice was deep and strong, his speech soft and gentle; and this contrast was carried through everything. He was totally courteous, a gentle-man by instinct as well as by tradition, and this imparted a grace to a strong, stocky body that would otherwise have seemed clumsy, with thick, muscular limbs. 'I'm almost as much round the calf of my leg as I am round the neck,' he remarked once. 'It's a dreadful deformity.'

It was typical of Nevill Coghill's extravagant humility that he should describe himself as having a deformity of any kind; in fact, he was more endowed with grace of manner and of mind than anyone I ever met, and this imparted itself even to his rather bear-like physique. It was one of the things that marked him off from the other Oxford dons of his, and I suppose of any, period. While most of them, as was natural, were English middle-class achievers who had gone up the educational ladder by cannily directed industry, Nevill was a scion of the Anglo-Irish Protestant gentry. Nowadays these people have a bad name; landowners are not in favour, and their characteristic recreations, such as fox-hunting, are likewise unpopular. During Nevill's lifetime the Ascendency, as it was once called, just about ceased to have any power or influence in Irish life (he

himself referred to it as 'the Descendency') and one never seems
to hear anyone regretting its disappearance. Yet Nevill, unless
he was a totally unique individual, is useful testimony that there
was another side to the picture. And surely he was not entirely
unique. Those declining landowners in their peeling stuccoed
houses, with their inefficiently farmed estates, fighting year by
year a losing battle with hard-faced officials in Dublin, were
after all the people who befriended Yeats and made his mature
work possible, not only by material support in the form of
hospitality but by providing a sympathetic *milieu* for his vision
of life moulded by style and tradition:

> A spot whereon the founders lived and died
> Seemed once more dear than life; ancestral trees,
> Or gardens rich in memory glorified
> Marriages, alliances and families
> And every bride's ambition satisfied.
> Where fashion or mere fantasy decrees
> We shift about – all that great glory spent –
> Like some poor Arab tribesman and his tent.

Nevill Coghill came from this background; I have no idea
whether his family's position in it was higher or lower than
Augusta Gregory's, but it was the world of his beginnings, and
in the world of our beginnings we put together our attitudes to
life, never to depart from them. He had a lack of competitive-
ness, an absence of the need to score points and shoot people
down, which characterised his work and his relationships
throughout a long life. By the time he arrived in Oxford at the
end of the First World War, he had behind him the boyhood
and adolescence typical of his class and generation – in other
words, Public School and then the trenches – but his formative
influences were unlike theirs in other respects. Ireland, especially in the years before 1914, was still inhabited by a peasantry
who believed in leprechauns and witches and the ever-present
Good People, and still handed down tales of ancient heroic
deeds; on the country roads there still wandered half-crazed

beggars of the type Yeats brought into his poetry as powerful symbols. Walking alone one day, Coghill's mother saw an old beggar-woman such as the poet had in mind when, many years later, he wrote the Crazy Jane poems. She approached with trepidation, for she knew the old woman would ask for alms and she had no money with her. Old beggar-women were notorious for putting a curse on passers-by who did not relieve their distress. But when their eyes met, and the anxious lady explained that her purse was empty, the crone reassured her with a gentle smile and the words, ''Tis not for the lucre of a penny that you and I will be fallin' out.'

This 'unbought grace of life', which some thought in those days ran through the whole Irish people from top to bottom, was evident in Nevill. When I first became acquainted with him, I knew nothing of all this; I did not know he had an Irish background, and if I had known I would not have known what to deduce from it, since I knew nothing about Ireland either Catholic or Protestant, and nothing of its civilisation; I suppose I had just about heard of Yeats and Synge, but certainly not of Lady Gregory. All I knew, as an English schoolboy coming up to Oxford from the most provincial of the provinces, was that Nevill, as an individual, was different in a number of ways from the other individuals who surrounded him, and that I instinctively liked these differences.

He was never my teacher – officially, that is – though I learnt more from him than from almost anyone. I got to know him because I was interested in the theatre and hoped I might get a part in one of his Shakespearean productions. And here again we must take a background glance. Nevill's productions of Shakespeare were very much a bone of contention in the Oxford of his day, or at any rate in the English Faculty. Puritan dislike of the theatre, well marked in Shakespeare's own lifetime, survived in various forms certainly until my young days. There may not actually have been Nonconformist deacons who considered the theatre the Devil's temple, but there were certainly academics, and professional scholars of English at that, who felt uneasy and disapproving when the study of drama, of drama however lofty, moved out of the library and into the theatre. Nevill Coghill, working with the Oxford University Dramatic Society, brought play after play to life by his summer productions, over a period of something like thirty years. These productions had to be in the open air, since Oxford at that time had no theatre that he could get his hands on, and the College halls were too small for productions as ambitious as his, and audiences (he hoped) as large. So the College gardens were used, and while there was undeniably a charm in seeing and hearing young people speaking these immortal lines against a background of such beauty, it was not the kind of setting in which a tradition can grow up, since each new production was at a different *venue* and the lessons of experience could not be applied. (Cambridge, which at least had the A.D.C. building, has produced far more men and women of the theatre than Oxford, in our century.)

But I digress. What offended the academic establishment about Nevill's productions was not their makeshift quality, the hit-or-miss flavour of the acting, the rainstorms which frequently drowned them out, and the general idea of flying blind and trusting to God; it was the very idea that a don should be mixed up in undergraduate theatricals at all. As an escapade now and again it might be pardonable. But Nevill made it an important component, perhaps the single most important, in his work as a teacher of literature. Summer after summer, he put across his interpretations of Shakespeare by staging the plays. And if the audiences went along for an evening's diversion and mostly got nothing much beyond that, it was a different story with the youths and girls who actually took part in these productions, who studied and rehearsed under Nevill's gentle but watchful eye and who became, during those eight weeks, steeped in Nevill's vision of that particular play. I know because I was one of them.

The official view in the English Faculty, I suppose, was that they remembered all too vividly the long struggle to get

'English' accepted as an academic study at all; and having finally levered it in, and still having to face a great deal of condescension about its being too soft an option, they had to show a grave face to the world, and that grave face simply did not go with dressing up and putting on grease-paint and capering about, even in *Hamlet*, even in the pouring rain which at any rate ensured that the experience was not remotely like fun.

Or perhaps they did not think these thoughts consciously at all, perhaps the chicken came before the egg, perhaps they were just the kind of people who would naturally, in such a situation, find themselves representing English literary studies at an ancient University; staid, prudent, ready to undertake labours of severe scholarship, but very suspicious of their *métier* at the points where it seemed to link up with the performing arts and with anything that looked like show business. Certainly the holder at that time of the Merton Chair of English, in Oxford the figure-head of the subject, would not deign to go and see Nevill's production of *The Two Gentlemen of Verona* when his own daughter was in it.

At all events, it was Nevill's practice of staging Shakespeare that led to my being acquainted with him; led me, that is, to tread the stairs to his rooms in Exeter College one crisp sunny day in the autumn of 1943. I knocked, obeyed his summons to come in, and found myself immediately in a different world from any I had known. The only other dons' rooms I had been in, those of my tutor and my moral tutor, were, essentially, libraries. The wall space was given to tightly crammed bookshelves, and the rest of the furniture was strictly utilitarian and distinctly well-used. My moral tutor, who had visited China, had brought back a fine silk screen which he used to shield him from draughts during those coal-less wartime winters, but otherwise there was nothing that appeared to have been chosen with an eye to its aesthetic qualities. Nevill's room immediately proclaimed itself as a different kind of place. Higgledy-piggledy with books and papers it may have been, but it was also

dominated by a large grand piano, on which stood an impressive bust of Nevill himself, and in the window-ledges were some
large, handsome drinking-glasses of a rich blue, through which
the afternoon sun glowed festively. Nevill's personality, as he
rose from his armchair to greet me, confirmed the impression
that here was a new and larger dimension, something that
opened windows on to a world beyond the University world of
study and meditation without turning its back on that world.
His manner, though not egalitarian, was genial, based on the
assumption that we were fellow-artists, in search of the same
ultimate goals of beauty and significance. When I say that his
manner was not egalitarian I mean that it was fatherly or
elder-brotherly rather than matey and all-boys-together. Even
when, a little later, he came with a gang of us to Stratford to
spend a week seeing as much Shakespeare as possible, and slept
in hideous discomfort in our bunk-room at the Youth Hostel,
he was totally friendly and approachable without ever taking on
the protective colouring of One of Us. The lady who ran the
Youth Hostel called him, half mockingly, 'the Dean and the
Don', and certainly he never made any effort not to be the dean
and the don. His object in coming along with us, his object in
assembling us for casting meetings, rehearsals, productions,
was not to confuse his own status with ours but to share an
experience – and in that sharing to forget all distinctions of
generation and rank. He was a Christian, and perhaps this made
it easier, since Christianity also inculcates the forgetting of rank
and position in the sharing of a common ideal, though one
would hardly think so from the way many avowed Christians
behave.

My early memories of Nevill are all intertwined with my
memories of Oxford summers, moist, green, and loud with
bird-song; those afternoons when he would sit in a chair in the
garden, a book and a sheaf of notes on his knee, usually a pipe
lying beside the chair half-buried in the fragrant grass, taking us
patiently through some scene, working hard but always with
time for a joking aside and a laugh – his laugh was like the rest of

his vocal utterance, rough by nature but gentle in its effect. And the conversation that bubbled about these experiences, before and after the spells of work, was always the conversation of someone to whom all the arts were real, and all equally loopholes to the world of the spirit. Nevill was a great celebrator. His heart was naturally full of the emotion of gratitude. The greatness of a Shakespeare or a Mozart or a Cézanne was to him simply an instance of the bounty of God, like the rain and the sun.

Not that he enjoyed them in a merely open-mouthed way. To him, they were there to be understood, and to understand them, to put yourself in a position to begin understanding them, called for work and discipline. I don't think even Nevill's detractors ever denied that he had a first-rate mind. He was a populariser in the sense that he tried to make the experience of the arts available to ordinary people who had not spent a lifetime studying them, but that did not mean that he himself shirked the obligation to spend a lifetime studying them. In token of which, I cite the fact that just about his first published contribution to the study of English literature was a celebrated essay on *Piers Plowman*, which appeared in the Oxford periodical *Medium Aevum* in 1933 and succeeded in explaining certain features of that great but baffling poem in a new yet satisfying way. To tackle *Piers Plowman* is not work for an amateur. It calls not only for a thorough knowledge of fourteenth-century English, but of the theology of mediaeval Catholicism: you have to keep one eye on Dante and Aquinas and the other on English literary tradition with poems like *Wynnere and Wastoure* and even *Gawain*. Nevill's essay broke new ground in that it ceased to see Langland's peom as a collection of fragments jammed into a rough whole, but credited it with a coherent structure and explained that structure by assuming that the character of Piers Plowman was intended as a three-stage allegory in which Piers is successively Do-Wel, Do-Bet and Do-Best. To recover this way of reading, after nearly three centuries in which allegory had been regarded as a dead letter, was both a scholarly and an imaginative break-through.

Nevill was on top of this kind of work not only because of the solidity of his base in that wide reading, but because of the rapid assimilative power of his mind. He was one of that post-War generation who took their basic training in some other subject (in his case, history) and then added the English School as a kind of top-dressing, reading what was normally a three-year course in one year and still getting a First. My point is not simply to insist on his excellent professional qualifications – it shouldn't be necessary to do more than take that for granted, with a don, though unfortunately it *is* sometimes necessary – as to defend Nevill against the persistent smear that he somehow wasted or trifled away what he had. The solid achievements are there. In particular his interest in *Piers Plowman* continued all his life; when, many years later, he lectured on the poem to the British Academy, he prepared so much material that the lecture as delivered from the platform had to be a mere running selection from the text, which amounted almost to a short book.

One always knew, then, even in youth, that in dealing with Nevill one was dealing with a serious, productive mind, as well as with a feaster and celebrator; that there were depths below the geniality and the sense of movement and colour and fun. And besides there was the matter of Nevill's Secret Sorrows. One was always being given to understand, in half-spoken rumours and head-shaking silences, that Nevill had Secret Sorrows of unusual dimensions. Some catastrophe had over-whelmed his life; perhaps before it happened his manner had not had that undercurrent of gentleness and suffering that occas-ionally made itself felt. He had, as a matter of public know-ledge, got married towards the end of the 1920s and set up home on Boar's Hill, and the marriage had ended five years later in divorce. The only reference I ever heard him make to it was when he said to me, laughing ruefully, 'My mother-in-law said to me "Never darken my door again" – she actually used those words!' Why a man with Nevill's good qualities should have been told not to darken someone's door again was, and is, a mystery to me, but I never troubled to enquire into it, preferring to take the man as I found him, and knowing how an unhappy marriage relationship can make people behave uncharacteristically. There was a permanent rumour that Nevill was homosexual, but in thirty years of knowing him, and knowing scores of people who also knew him, I never came across one piece of concrete evidence of this, even hearsay evidence. In any case, during the long period when I knew him well, his life evidently contained no amatory element at all. He lived in College, and at the end of his working life he retired into the country with his elder brother. It was very much a bachelor existence, except that Nevill was not like the usual crusted academic bachelor, keeping himself to himself in a set of rooms and staring out into the silent quadrangle. He seemed always to be in touch with life.

Certainly his unassuming friendliness, and his kindliness, laid him open to experiences that hardly come within the life-pattern of the average don. I remember his telling me of one such. He was walking back late one night to his College when a disconsolate man stopped him and asked if he knew anywhere to get a bed for the night. The man was, it appeared, a lorry driver who had made some kind of mistake or met with some kind of delay, and found himself in the middle of Oxford with no idea where to sleep. Nevill, instead of uttering some vague formula and passing on, said that the man might come along and sleep on his sofa, which would at least be better than standing outside in the weather. They went to Nevill's rooms, he showed the lorry driver the sofa, and before they retired poured out a bottle of beer and paused a few minutes in talk. It soon became clear that the man found Oxford totally mysterious; he had no idea what it was all supposed to be for. 'Well, you see,' said Nevill, 'it's a kind of school, and I'm one of the teachers.' The man digested this and then said, 'Well, sir, if you're a teacher, perhaps you can answer a question for me.' 'What is it?' 'What were the causes of the Reformation?' Nevill was, obviously, somewhat taken aback at this question thrown so suddenly into their talk, but he did his best, as they sat with their beer, to rough out why the Reformation had become necessary and by what stages it came about. The lorry driver listened carefully and then said, 'Oh, I see. I'm glad you could tell me that. You see, I'm a Protestant and I've got a mate who's a Catholic, and he keeps on telling me that the only reason Henry the Eighth left the Church of Rome was because he wanted to get divorced and have another woman. And I've never liked the thought that my religion is all along of another man's wickedness.'

This little incident happened after Nevill had been made Merton Professor and had left Exeter for Merton. His election to this, the senior post in English Literature in Oxford, was not unanimous; there was an anti-Coghill faction, one of whose principals, a woman, made a great deal of difficulty for him during all the years he held the Chair by an attitude of vicious hostility and non-cooperation. For myself, I was glad to see him in that position. The age of the hard-nosed professionals was already upon us (the year was 1956) and scholars of Nevill's type, who still kept some roots in the epoch when literature was regarded as an art rather than simply the raw material of an industry, were going into their sunset. And of course Nevill had against him not only his involvement in University drama, not only his venture into production on the West End stage, but, in the 1950s, another career as the intermediary between the work of Chaucer and the large public who, while ready for his humour and pathos and wisdom, would never have taken the trouble to read him in Middle English. Nevill translated Chaucer, deftly and gracefully, into modern rhyming verse and took a major hand in producing its recital over the air; in fact I would say that his Chaucer readings were among the triumphs of the early days of the Third Programme, in its palmy days before radio was backed into a corner by television. (A very fertile corner it has proved to be; but still, a corner.)

Needless to say the academic establishment, none of whom

could have brought off the feat of translating Chaucer into easily-flowing modern verse without spilling a drop of his essence, were darkly disapproving of Nevill's enterprise. He also had, in those strait-laced days, his battles with the B.B.C. on that side which has earned her the affectionate name of 'Auntie'. Chaucer's poetry goes over the whole range of feeling and expression, from lofty idealism to the ultimate in earthiness, and in a decade that still retained some traces of nineteenth-century prudery this earthiness presented certain problems in polite society. Nevill, translating *The Canterbury Tales* for radio, had a particularly hard struggle with that sudden outburst of angry scurrility when the Host, outraged by the Pardoner's brazen admission of hypocrisy and cynicism, assails him with a storm of insults, culminating in

> I wolde I hadde thy coillons in myn hond
> In stede of relikes or of seintuarie;
> Lat cutte hem of, I wol thee helpe hom carie;
> Thay shul be shryned in an hogges tord.

One evening of wind and rain I bumped into Nevill striding back from the railway station towards College after a day in the studios. His version of the first of those lines, beginning 'I would I had thee by the balls', had been censored out; he had been forced to compromise with 'I would I had thee by the bowels'. (An equally horrible thought, surely.) He told me about this, puffing with laughter, then, as he walked rapidly away down the windy street, his voice came back to me through the darkness as he called over his shoulder the consoling afterthought, 'But I got away with the hog's turd!'

I have said that Neville's personality and life-style were a revelation to me in adolescence, supplying an element that was otherwise lacking in the Oxford I knew. They went on supplying that element until I was well into my forties. There were plenty of pleasant and interesting people about, but it was to Nevill that one turned at any heightened moment, when something happened that demanded celebration. When Toby, the only one of our sons to have been born in Oxford, made his appearance in the maternity wing of the Radcliffe Infirmary one May morning in 1966, I found myself outside in the street, knowing that all was well but under instructions not to come back till two o'clock. Where did my feet take me? Obviously, to Merton and up the stairs to Nevill's room. He had someone with him – Nevill always had someone with him – but he dived into the cupboard for a bottle of champagne, and he and I and the other man (whose name and face I have forgotten, and I apologise to him for it) celebrated the miracle of birth with the other miracles of good wine and good friendship.

So it had been through the years, and so it continued to be, and it never occurred to me to try to imagine Oxford without him. I knew, of course, as an intellectual fact, that he would one day retire, and had heard him speak of settling in the Gloucestershire countryside. But I found a Nevill-less Oxford so totally unimaginable that I never even pictured it.

And then, one June evening, the truth that I had evaded sought me out, as truths will. My wife and I had gone to bed unusually early, while it was still light, and as I sank to sleep she roused me to say that there was somebody moving about downstairs. Warm and comfortable, I mumbled that if some tramp had got in to go to sleep by the fire we ought to leave him in peace. I meant, of course, leave *me* in peace. But as the sounds from downstairs continued, I came back to wakefulness and decided to investigate. Dressing-gowned, I went down. There, by the greying log fire, were Nevill and the inevitable Someone He Had With Him, in this case a young man with whom he had been dining at some country inn. Obviously as they drove back into Oxford, approaching it from the north, Nevill had remembered the Wains and decided to call in.

I put some more logs on the fire and we sat and had the last of those hundreds of talks – easy, flowing, sharing of ideas. It was not the last time I saw him; he came to Oxford now and then during his retirement, and I would sometimes run into him; but these would be brief meetings in a corridor or on the steps of a building. This was the last leisurely time. Nevill told me that he was busy packing and was leaving Oxford the next day, and then he and the young man got into their car and drove off. As I climbed the stairs I knew at last that he had gone.

'Of course,' said the lady who found herself sitting next to me at a lunch-party, the wife of some academic, 'I always understood that Nevill Coghill was just a caretaker as Merton Professor.' She meant no harm, she was merely repeating the small-talk of the profession, what little Professor Wubb and Dr Glubb have told each other is the right thing to say about Nevill. I informed her briefly that Nevill was the best Merton Professor Oxford had ever had or was likely to have; and for the rest of the meal I was largely silent, not because I was sulking but because I was remembering Nevill, his courtesy, his generosity, his sensibility, his wit, his kindliness. Yes, he was a caretaker, and never was such care taken.

Julia

TO COME ACROSS a character like Julia in a Warwickshire village was a strange, contradictory experience; on the one hand purely surprising, yet on the other entirely natural, since she was as believable, as solid, as inevitable as Dogberry or Mistress Quickly. And yet she resembled neither of these so much as she resembled a female version of the great Falstaff himself. Or perhaps, with her unquenchable oddity, she would have had to be invented, if she had been a fictitious character, by some connoisseur of the quirkiness of humanity rather than a writer of Shakespeare's centrality. One could imagine meeting her in the pages of *Tristram Shandy*. Yet her historical period, the scenes of her adventures, were substantially those of Gerald du Maurier's *Trilby* or even Murger's *Vie de Bohême*.

After that rapid fire of literary allusions, entirely appropriate in introducing a person so highly charged with imagination, so accustomed to seeing her own life as a collection of legends that she never troubled to narrate, let us draw breath and come at the subject more factually. Julia's origins were Birmingham Irish. She had grown up in Shirley, where her father had kept, I think, a livery stable. Someone told me once that Julia as a girl used to help to break in horses; if so, this might have brought her into contact with circus and fairground people and perhaps started her on that lifelong association, in one form and another, with show business and the performing arts.

At all events, when I got to know her in the early to middle 1940s she must have been over sixty; so that the version of her history most generally accepted, that she had been an artist's model in Paris at the turn of the century, squared perfectly well with chronology. I say 'generally accepted' because it was the version current among most people who knew her, though where they got it I am not sure, since Julia herself never mentioned her own past history except very rarely in a brief aside. But she certainly knew Paris, and her memories of it seemed to be from that epoch and from the angle of vision, so to speak, that would be natural to a Birmingham girl who was modelling for a living and mixing with a Bohemian, largely English-speaking, set. She referred now and then to Parisian buildings and institutions, but always gave them their names in English – 'Oh, yes, that was in a little street over by the Red Windmill.'

A girl from a Shirley livery stable who became a favourite of the artists' community in the Paris of 1900 must be presumed to have had something to offer, and perhaps the young Julia had been a beauty. When I first saw Julia I was nineteen, an age at which one does not think of people over forty as having physical lives at all, or even much in the way of a physical appearance beyond what will serve to tell one apart from another. They are, to the eyes of an adolescent as to the eyes of a child, rather like life-size animated dolls: always clothed, needless to say, and always in very much the same *kind* of clothes; and always moving, sitting or standing in characteristic attitudes. Their individuality comes partly from the way they move their limbs and even more from the sound of their voices. If you hear a young person talking about an older one – a schoolboy, say, relating some encounter with a master – the voice will always be mimicked, and nearly always in grotesque caricature.

So, at nineteen, I did not think of Julia as 'looking like' anything in particular, and certainly not as being beautiful or ugly. Her voice, which was cheerful and penetrating, was somewhat battered (what people called a 'whisky voice', which she had certainly taken steps to earn) but had clarity in its middle range, and must at one time have been melodious. In build she was of medium height for a woman, and, though by this time rather dumpy, she was supple and active enough. What strikes me, looking back, is that her head and face were, in fact, beautiful, with that beauty which is not affected by age because it is a matter of bone structure, and carriage, and expression. Her iron-grey hair was wound round her head in some sort of long plait, giving a helmetlike impression that carried a hint of the classical; she could have posed for a statue of Minerva. As for her face, its features were good; the nose in particular, straight and delicate, gave her refinement, a touch of the human thoroughbred.

I forgive my nineteen-year-old self, however, for not taking much notice of Julia's face, because one eye was covered by a large black patch, looped round her head with elastic. I suppose she found this more comfortable than a glass eye, and certainly the socket behind it was empty. So one tended, on catching sight of her face, to have one's attention drawn straight to the patch; and what remained of her girlish beauty, for surely it had once been fresh and vivid, went unnoticed.

As for how she came by the patch, once again her *milieu* had an accepted story: the eye had been shot out at the gaming table in Monte Carlo. Later I heard another version that laid the scene in Dieppe; a reckless, distraught gambler had pulled out a revolver and taken a shot at someone, the bullet had ricocheted and entered Julia's eye, whereupon Julia's escort had pulled out his own revolver and shot the man dead on the spot. Heady stuff, not normally associated with Warwickshire village life – the splendid, sinewy raw material of legend.

Meanwhile, what was I, at nineteen, doing in this *galère*? The answer is in one magic word, 'Shakespeare'. That poet has had a great influence on my life. Not only have I spent substantial amounts of time studying his work and writing about it, not only have I at times earned an income by talking about it to students and actors and actresses; it has been the magnet that has drawn me into many places and many relationships. I could run through a whole list of people I would never have known had they and I not shared an involvement with Shakespeare and a love of him. I would never have trodden Nevill Coghill's staircase and introduced myself to him if he had not been casting one of his productions of Shakespeare. I would never have formed my youthful friendship with Richard Burton. I would never have met George Rylands at Cambridge, or a whole string of Stratford players through the years.

Julia is a name in that list, though like the others she very soon took on a life of her own. I wanted to see as many Shakespearean plays as I could, and my initial reason for coming into contact with Julia was that she kept 'theatrical lodgings'. This, I fancy, is a trade that has now pretty well disappeared. In Victorian times the lower reaches of the acting profession lived a life that one would not have expected any human being to stand for, as long as there was a ditch to dig. Every town of any size had a theatre; most theatres were played by little fit-up companies who performed for one week – six evening shows and at least one matinee – and, on the Sunday morning, packed up and travelled on. Each Sunday, the country must have been threaded in every direction by touring theatrical companies, stage managers loading props in the guard's van, producers gloomily adding up the budget, bravely joking and chattering and keeping up each other's spirits as they waited on foggy platforms or clattered past silent goods yards. On arrival, there was no time to look for somewhere to stay. The theatre would have the addresses of landladies in the neighbouring streets – because there was no time, either, for long journeys to and from the suburbs – who let rooms to 'theatricals', one lot going and another lot coming in the way the tide fills and washes out a rock-pool. The English theatre, and its red-nosed half-sister Twice-Nightly Variety, were made possible for a hundred years by this army of theatrical landladies, many or most of whom were superannuated dancers or singers, or the widows of jugglers or conjurors or female impersonators. They have departed – unsung, as far as I know, and unhonoured – into the shades of history.

I am the more glad to have known, in Julia, a particularly fine, though late-blooming, specimen of the type. Not that she let rooms by the week. Her cottage was at Shottery, very near Anne Hathaway's, and Stratford-on-Avon dealt with no weekly touring fit-up companies. Her *clientèle* were Shakespearean actors and actresses, who took their rooms for 'the season'. But they represented the most modest level of the company, mostly employed to carry a spear or make one of a colourful whirling crowd; or they were wardrobe staff, or they painted scenery or did general odd jobs. I remember, for instance, a boy who worked in the wardrobe department, cutting out costumes and allowed occasionally to put in a suggestion as to their design. I never knew anyone, male or female, as deeply devoted to clothes as this youth. There was a gleam of pure happiness in his eye as he talked of the wonderful outfits they contrived. He told me once about the dress they had made for that year's leading lady (it was Diana Wynyard): 'A lovely creation', he called it, 'in stinging cerise.' I went to the theatre and hardly attended to the play. Every time Diana Wynyard made an entrance a voice in my head intoned, 'a lovely creation in stinging cerise.'

At Julia's, one met small-part actors, young ones who hoped they were on the way up and old ones who feared they were on the way down, and stage-management staff, and even people like me, for my friends and I used to get over from Oxford when we could, and during these years I saw some sort of production of all Shakespeare's major plays. The Stratford Memorial Theatre, though even then a national institution, was not so grand in those days as it has since become; it had some help from public funds, but not on the gargantuan scale it has since come to expect, and in the winter it closed down for months on end. Closed down as a Shakespearean theatre, that is; it showed variety and pantomime, and I have stayed at Julia's with red-nosed comics, girl tap-dancers, and one young man who went on to become solidly established as a player of the mouth organ (sorry, harmonica). Then there was the pair of male lovers who kept a market-garden. (Did their establishment not contain any living accommodation? Why were they at Julia's? Or did they just come for meals?) And there was the middle-aged man with the withered hand and the courteous, cultivated manner, who appeared to live mainly on, and for, gin, and was said to disappear on three- or four-day blinds at the end of which some policeman would gather up his unconscious body from a gutter. There was the young actor who always referred to everyone at the theatre, male or female, as 'a screaming bitch' and shortly afterwards crossed the Atlantic and embarked on a well-publicised affair with a Hollywood actress, which made the headlines in the cheap Sunday papers for month after month. And the slightly less young actor who, worried about his fast-dwindling hair, had heard or read somewhere that nettle-stings brought the moribund roots back to life. He used to go out of the front door, walk a few steps to where there was a thick bed of nettles, go down on his hands and knees and sting his bald dome stoically at least once a day. I have seen him on the stage since, but whether wigged or not I could not tell.

Over this motley, shifting empire Julia presided, and it must be said that one thing they had in common was unwavering loyalty to her. Every human being encounters dislike and hostility sometimes, but if anyone disliked Julia they must have kept well away from Stratford, for I never met or heard of them. By the sheer force of her character, starting with no material advantages – for after all she was just a rather battered woman on the far side of middle age, in a shabby dress and an eye-patch, who kept a boarding house – she established total authority in her circle. And she did it, as I say, without making enemies. She simply drew you into her world; and once you were in her world you paid homage to her because she was queen of it.

And what was Julia's world? It was, I can see now, a very Celtic dimension. She had the gift of surrounding ordinary humdrum life with an atmosphere of celebration. She loved fantasy and humour, and her chief instrument for projecting them was verbal. Her vocabulary was made up of dozens of ritual phrases. Nothing was called by its ordinary name. In particular the basic facts of existence were given labels that coloured them with a mocking humour. To die was 'to pass down the tramcar'. Somebody with bad lungs was 'coughing his soul-case up'. The lavatory out in the backyard was 'the Palace of Varieties' or more simply 'the Palace'.

This verbal gossamer became entangled with everything. A perfectly ordinary woman called Mrs Nichols, who lived near-by, was always 'My Lady Nicotine'. (The reference is to a now forgotten book by J. M. Barrie.) If she expressed her intention of going down to The Bell to have a whisky, it was always 'a little whixey-itis'. If this sounds arch, I can only say that in its effect it was nothing of the kind. Julia was far too earthy to be arch. Though, speaking of earthiness, I believe it is a fact worth recalling that I never heard her use a single one of the official rude words. The content of what she said may have come from the world of Émile Zola's Parisian back streets and Murger's studios, but the vocabulary would not have offended a Victorian governess.

At first, Julia must have seen me as one more faceless lodger coming in and going out with the tide, but our relationship became closer when she realised that I shared her gift for fanciful talk. On one of my earliest visits, the cottage must have been crowded, because I was sleeping on a camp-bed in the kitchen, and was awakened in the early morning by a young cat, barely out of kittenhood, treading warily and delicately over me. Frail, skinny, pacing very scrupulously on long white legs, the little cat reminded me, as I said to Julia at breakfast-time, of 'a ballerina who was new to the job.' Julia instantly seized on the phrase, the cat was known as 'the ballerina' for the rest of its life, and I became in her mind an identifiable person.

For me, Julia's cottage, number something, Hathaway Hamlet, Shottery – it torments me that I cannot remember the number, and if I go back to look now the changed appearance of the place confuses me and I am not sure which door was Julia's – the cottage, I say, held a very special place at the centre of my affections and of my imaginative world. What appealed to me was the blend of the rural with the artistic, intellectual, Bohemian. I was well enough accustomed to country life, and already my love of the countryside had formed its deep roots, but I had made very few close relationships with actual country people, whose talk of crops and the weather and subsidies tended necessarily to exclude me. I knew a number of families who ran small farms on the borders of Staffordshire and Shropshire; I liked and respected them, and they were kind to me; but this was not the sort of ground from which real friendships grow. At Julia's I found a rural environment, a thatched cottage among a cluster of such cottages at the end of a tree-lined lane – and inside the cottage, talk of the theatre and books and music, and gossip about wonderfully exciting people, and, yes, even lovely creations in stinging cerise.

Perhaps it all sounds silly and juvenile, but as the French poet remarked, *Tant pis, c'est moi*. That vision of life has remained with me always as an ideal. You can tell everything about a person by finding out his or her notion of happiness. All of us, I think, carry about in the back of our minds a vision of what the truly happy life would be, if we could only attain it. The degree to which this vision is blurred or precise will vary greatly from one mind to another, but I believe it is always there. My vision of happiness has always been a life in which there is the excitement of ideas, the divine rage of art and the self-forgetfulness of the artist, set amid quiet fields and gardens and trees, with a river winding somewhere nearby. I have the temperament of an artist, the absolute need to live my life in a continuum of art and ideas as well as of experiences; but, in my century, these things have nearly always had to be sought in the big cities of the world, where noise and haste and crowded pavements give a hysterical edge to life and therefore increasingly to art.

It was not always so. Goethe's Weimar, Mozart's Salzburg, were small, meadowy towns. Shakespeare's London, though it had its dark and dangerous places, must have had quiet lanes where the country people drove their flocks exactly as they did in Stratford. How big was the Florence of Dante or even the Paris of Villon? Great art, great ideas, have flowered from small towns that grew like trees, with their roots in the soil and their branches spread to the sky. I know historically, from the kind of examples I have just given, that this wise and fortunate balance was possible, that it has been a reality in human life; and I know personally, within my own life-experience, what it felt like; because that was what life at Julia's felt like.

Sometimes one sees a fisherman's cottage right down on the beach, so close to the sea that one might think the next high wave would engulf it; but of course the wisdom and local knowledge of the builder has put it for ever just out of reach of the biggest rollers. Julia's cottage, and Hathaway Hamlet generally, were in this position *vis-à-vis* the perpetually incoming tide of tourists and sightseers. No one who has been on so much as a day trip to Stratford will need to be told that Anne Hathaway's cottage is situated in Shottery, about a mile from the centre of town, to be reached either by walking across the fields or going round by the road. The coaches and cars go round by the road, and in those days the road that ran past the cottage was a *cul-de-sac*; people stopped, got out, and did the official visit, or merely stared at the building from the roadway and crossed it off their list, and drove back the way they had come. The fifty yards surrounding Anne's birthplace marked the end of that particular tourist run. If the visitors had gone another two hundred yards down the road, they would have came upon this cluster of thatched and half-timbered dwellings, all the same period as Anne's, and no doubt their cameras would have been clicking and whirring. But they never did. The next destination was waiting, the next item to be crossed off the list, and the tide, after each toppling wave, receded.

Apart from that one manifestation of the sightseeing trade, life in Shottery, in the 1940s and early 1950s, was very quiet and untroubled. House prices and rents were still low. The village inn, The Bell, was still an ordinary country pub.

Needless to say, things are very different now. To mention only two changes in particular, the road running past Anne Hathaway's is no longer a dead end; it runs on and links up with one of the main roads in and out of Stratford, so that there is always the sound of traffic; and the Bell Inn has expanded for a mass *clientèle* who would leave no room for a Julia sitting comfortably at the bar with her whixey-itis. Hathaway Hamlet, for its part, has obviously become the estate agent's dream it was always destined to be.

I knew Julia well for, I suppose, seven or eight years. During that time my vision of her naturally became clearer and more rounded. I was growing up, and she was revealing more of herself. My first impressions of her were two-dimensional, as a richly funny character, full of quirks and peculiarities, hovering several feet above ordinary mundane life in the same way that Falstaff does. But Falstaff, in the end, is punctured and brought down to earth; and Julia ultimately revealed, to my wondering young eyes, that she was a real woman and not a character from some rich, bubbling picaresque novel; that she had, like everyone else, a relationship with the ordinary world in all its dailiness and predictability.

It was, of course, a relationship of adversaries. The ordinary daily world is not friendly to those who live outside its enclosures. At worst it persecutes them into isolation, madness, and death. At best it denies them the solid satisfactions that are its own comforts and compensations. Julia had (evidently) parted company with the conventional world at the very beginning of her life, and the world had, as usual, exacted its price. She had been made to suffer. I never, of course, learned the history of these sufferings, but as I grew to know her better I had occasional glimpses into the depths of her resentments, resentments that could only have arisen from pain, exclusion, humiliation. She hated, for instance, anything to do with established religion. I must have been staying at the cottage one Christmas, because although I don't remember anything else about it I remember sitting in front of the fire on Christmas Eve, listening on the radio to the carol service from King's College, Cambridge. At least, I started to listen to it, but Julia, who was moving about attending to various household tasks, began to show signs of discomfort and nervous impatience. The clerical tones, the soaring voices of the choirboys, seemed to cause her a distress similar to that suffered by a person who can't bear a cat in the room and suddenly sees one come in. 'Bosh and bad luck!' she hissed, flicking venomously at the radio with a duster as she went past. 'Bosh and bad luck, that is!' She did not actually seize the radio and switch it off, but I could see she was longing to, so I did it for her. To this day I listen on Christmas Eve to that carol service from King's, and to this day I hear Julia's 'bosh and bad luck' – the two have fused in my mind into an antiphonal whole.

Then, a year or two later, I was again sitting by the cottage fireside in the afternoon and Julia began talking about a man she had loved. I remember very few facts about this man and her relationship with him. Perhaps she gave me very few. But she had loved him and they had had wonderful times together. 'He had an old Riley car, and we used to go away for holidays, driving about wherever we took a fancy to go.' Was the man married? Was there some external reason why he and Julia could not settle down into a regular union, or was it just temperamental? At any rate: 'One Christmas he said to me, "My father wants me to go to Communion with him. And I can't." I said "Why not?" and he said "Because of you." So I said, "Well, if that's how you feel, you'd better get on with it." ' And that, I was left to gather, had been their parting.

So it came to me, in glimpses, a vision of the thorns that had beset Julia's path, how she had had her heart broken, been denied this and excluded from that.

I thought a good deal about Julia's lover, and his old Riley, and his churchgoing father. But the real food for thought came one chilly summer evening when, with the light fading behind the small leaded panes, Julia unexpectedly launched into a long string of stories, each one the case history of some person whose life had been spoilt by respectability, domesticity, marriage. She seemed to have known case after case of people, usually men but sometimes women too, who had lived under such tension in the prison-house of social conformity that they had ended up by going to pieces or doing desperate things. I sat, appalled, silently listening. 'They showed me all round their little new home, all set up with this and that and the flowers in the garden and a car in the garage. And I thought, "He's in his squirrel-cage. And he'd give his soul to get out of it." '

I shall never forget that evening: Julia's voice, drained now of its laughter and self-mockery, lowered to a flat and emphatic *timbre*, adding story to story of frustration and suffering. Every word entered my ear like a stab. For I, too, was in my squirrel-cage.

In recalling, here, my visits to Hathaway Hamlet I have consistently made use of the first person singular: *I* did this, *I* found that. Actually it was nearly always We. I had the company, most of the time, of the wife I married when I was twenty-two and parted from finally when I was thirty. I do not want to discuss this relationship beyond remarking that nothing in the whole awful mess was particularly my wife's fault. For me to get married at twenty-two was a monumental act of folly, and it was her misfortune (as well as, to a significant extent, her doing,) that I should have involved her in that folly.

Sometimes I look back on that wedding day in July, 1947, and try to reconstruct the state of mind that had driven me through all the stages – the proposal, the ring, the banns, culminating finally in that dazed walk down the aisle. It took place in St Giles's Church, Northampton, a few yards from Northampton General Hospital where John Clare found asylum during the long years of his madness; but he was not madder than I was.

I am; but what I am none cares or knows.

Looking back, I feel that that line applied as well to me on that July morning as it ever did to him. What could I have been thinking of? What kind of vision had I, if I had any at all, of the fifty more years I expected to live? I have lived nearly forty of them and, looking back, all I can say is that I see as little into the mind of that young man as if he were someone else, someone I never met or heard of.

The wedding ceremony – it took about ten minutes, in the almost empty church – seemed to snap the spell. At once, standing in the vestry, I knew the monstrous folly of what I had done. But it was too late. The register lay open for our names; the pen was handed to me with the ink wet on the nib. We signed, and a decade of disaster for both of us was under way.

Of the effect on my partner's life, I can say nothing, except that I think of her with total compassion. The effect on my life was, first, to ruin my twenties. My psychic maladjustment found expression in physical illness, and when I look back on that decade I see doctors' waiting rooms and hospital wards. Nor did the distortion stop there, because in my thirties, or at any rate the first half of them, I wasted a lot of energy having the sort of 'good time' I ought to have had ten years earlier and got out of the way.

Sometimes I wonder whether my trance-like state, the incredible lack of self-knowledge combined with zombie fatalism, did not result from some kind of deep exhaustion. Between seventeen and twenty-one I not only filled my head with an enormous amount of information, I also reoriented my life and therefore to some extent my personality. After growing up in Stoke-on-Trent and having no chance to absorb any but the notions of Stoke-on-Trent, I was pitchforked into Oxford at seventeen, and immediately recognised it as the natural setting for my life and endeavours. But there is a snag in that word 'natural.' If Oxford was my natural place, then Stoke-on-Trent had been artificial, and, since it had so totally moulded me, I had to break out of that mould, not with any overt feelings of hostility and rejection (if asked at any time of my life, I would always have said I liked Stoke, and so I did in very many ways) but with a long, dragging, unconscious effort, like the effort of a plant to turn round to a stronger source of light.

The quarrel, if such it was, is long since healed, and my two towns now seem to me each to have given me about half of my personality as it is today. But *something* must have put me into that drugged state, and perhaps it was that the long effort of adaptation had left me without the energy to steer a course through the maze of conflicting experiences that life in one's twenties always is.

I can see my wife now on that evening in Julia's cottage, sitting on a chair in the corner, a small dark figure with head bent, listening. And I can see myself, pale and wan, sitting aghast as Julia knocked out the props, one by one, from 'the old and bitter world where they marry in churches.' Julia, who had always been a builder of shelters, who had always fashioned beautiful and whimsical structures of fantasy and good humour in which one could pretend to be living one's life, was for that hour relentlessly destructive, heaping up story on story about people who had tried to ignore the needs of their emotions and instincts, tried to make themselves snug little shelters for the sake of safety and respectability and then found that the shelters were cages against which they must hurl themselves till something broke, they or the cage or both . . . I had gone, so often and so eagerly, to Hathaway Hamlet as a glorious playground, and now suddenly it was a house of correction.

I found growing up a long and painful process, so long that perhaps in the end I shall go down to the grave with the process still not completed. But I do at least know when it started: that rain-chilled evening, sitting wordless by the empty fireplace as Julia poured the cold torrent of her anger against settled people and their settled ways.

Arnold

ARNOLD was a citizen of Stoke-on-Trent. He was born there during the reign of Queen Victoria and he lived there for nearly eighty-one years. He died about ten years ago, but he does not seem, yet, to have started to be forgotten. I still meet people who remember him and like to recall him, some of them a long way from Stoke-on-Trent, and I am beginning to realise that I was not alone in finding him unusual and memorable.

He was a small man – five feet six inches – and rather skimpy in build, probably through not having enough to eat while he was growing. His nose was beaky (he preferred it to be called 'Roman'), his lips full, his blue eyes piercing and full of energy. His hair had probably been fair in his childhood but long before I knew him it had settled down to being an ordinary mouse-colour; by nature I would guess that it was rather unruly, but he kept it well cut and sternly plastered down. He could not have felt at ease with untidy hair any more than he could have felt at ease with clothes that were stained, or baggy, or torn. He was always what people call 'well turned out', and he walked with a brisk, alert step and generally gave an impression of prompt-ness, of being ready for anything, of rather welcoming the unexpected event that broke the pattern of dailiness. His voice was good and he spoke clearly and distinctly, though not slowly.

I do not know whether Arnold had any unusual gifts, but he was unusual in his energy, his positiveness and his unslackening interest in life. He opened his eyes on each new day with the attitude of a man entering on an inheritance. Another whole day! What a blessing – what a privilege!

I knew him for many years but I never once heard him say he was bored. The word did not seem to be in his vocabulary. Why should it be, when the concept was never real to his mind?

Arnold was born in one of a row of very poor cottages, long

since demolished, called Johnson's Terrace. They were at the bottom of Hartshill Bank, which means that of the six Pottery towns, not yet amalgamated into the city of Stoke-on-Trent, the one Arnold inhabited was Stoke itself. Though in 1910 it gave its name to the federation, Stoke was in fact one of the meanest and ugliest of this string of towns; Burslem had some approach to civic dignity and Hanley had the prosperous shops and the amusements, but Stoke had nothing but pot-banks and a dirty canal and narrow streets lined with low brick houses. The only building worth looking at twice was the large and handsome parish church, in whose yard Josiah Wedgwood was buried. Stoke had the railway, which was why the city was ultimately named after it, but it was not an important railway town like Crewe a few miles away over the Cheshire border. Stoke meant long hours of work, small pubs, pawnshops, football on Saturday afternoons and chapel on Sunday evening.

Arnold's family, oddly enough, were not Chapel. They were Church if they were anything, but mostly they were not anything. It is difficult to speak or to think of them collectively as a family; they were a jumble of individuals, who happened to live in the same cramped little house. Arnold's father had very little ambition to be the impressive head of a family. He was often out of work, and when he was in work he took care to spend a large proportion of his earnings on beer, which helped him to forget his surroundings. He was a skilful man in the pottery trade; one of his skills was that he could fire a kiln, which must have been very responsible work. The old bottle kilns had about half-a-dozen grates round their circumference, each one like an ordinary domestic fireplace, and you had to light all these and then keep them at a constant temperature for twelve hours – if you failed it cost the factory a lot of money and doubtless cost you your job. Arnold's father could do this and several other jobs on a pot-bank, and there was no reason why he should not have been in steady employment. No outside reason, that is; the reason was within himself. He could never bring himself to sign on for a job on a regular basis. He preferred to be hired by the day. Perhaps it gave him some small illusion of freedom, of being an independent spirit who could make up his mind each morning whether that day should be work or holiday. In fact, he always let luck, or other people, decide the matter; invariably, at six o'clock every morning, he would make his way to Campbell Place, the nearest approach in Stoke to a wide market square, and the foremen would come out from the surrounding factories and take on as many hands as they needed. His conditions of employment, in fact, were exactly those we read about in the Parable of the Vineyard.

Since he never saved any money, it was a thin day at home when he was not hired, and not much better when he was, for he preferred beer to food and did not see it as his concern to provide the latter in any abundance. When, later in his boyhood, Arnold began to earn a little money by running errands and the like, if the family meal included something filling like jam suet roll, he would buy his father's share from him for a penny.

A penny, in about 1905, would buy half a pint of beer, and it would be better beer than we can get today, so Arnold's father may well have preferred it to jam roll. He earned five shillings when he did a day's work; if he had drunk less and worked at all often this would have been enough even for that large family (parents, four boys and a girl), for prices were very low in those days. Arnold's mother could put a hot meal on the table for sixpence. She would go to the butcher's for 'four penn'orth of bits', the odds and ends that always result when meat is trimmed; the greengrocer would sell her a pennyworth each of potatoes and 'pot-herbs'; and, using the fire that in any case kept the family warm and dried their clothes, she made this tanner do its work of nourishment.

The trouble was there were too many days when even a tanner was too much to hope for. The couple's first-born, a boy named Will, lived with grandparents a few streets away; I never heard the exact reason for this, but it seems to indicate that they were having difficulty, right from the beginning, in making ends meet. Then came a girl, then two other boys, then Arnold; and when Arnold was three or four years old 'his nose was pushed out', as his mother did not fail to remark, by the arrival of one more offspring, Norman, the baby of the family.

The image she had in mind was of a row of piglets feeding. Not that there was ever much for Arnold's nose to be pushed out of. During one desperate winter, his mother went to the Town Hall to ask if any kind of relief was available. The official told her that nothing could be handed out, but if the family were destitute they could be admitted to the workhouse. Arnold remembered her coming home and laughing about this, though what she had to laugh at is more than I can see. Perhaps she laughed in order to stop herself from breaking down and crying all night.

When Arnold reached the age of five he was made free of the blessings of compulsory education, a great British innovation and at that time less than thirty years old. He went to Cross Street Elementary School, Stoke. On the first morning his grandmother carried him there on her shoulders, so that he would know the way there and back, and he cried all through the journey. What he had heard about school in advance, no doubt from his brothers, had not given him the impression that it was a happy place. In the very simple school organisation of those days, the children did not go to different teachers for different subjects: one teacher had charge of a class (it was called a 'Standard') for a year and they were then passed on in a body to another teacher. The man who was to be in charge of Arnold's standard for the next twelve months greeted them by showing them his cane and rasping, 'I'm Mr So-and-So. This is my cane. We're going to see who gets tired first – me of giving it to you or you of getting it.' He may have been intending a grim joke; if so, it was too grim for the nervous, downcast children ushered for the first time into the prison-like classroom. The next seven years, till at twelve he could finally get away from school, were misery for Arnold.

If school was miserable, home was not very cheerful either.

The poky, uncomfortable little house they lived in could doubtless be rented for half-a-crown a week, but to budget even this sum regularly was beyond the power of his father. They fell behind with the rent; in the dead of night they piled their belongings into a cart and moved to a new address. This process, the 'moonlight flit', was familiar enough in the poorer reaches of the working class in those days and for a long time afterwards. Since the removal was usually to somewhere within half a mile and everybody in the district knew everybody, you only got away with it if the landlord was prepared to be philosophical about writing off a bad debt rather than troubling to bring a prosecution. Landlords were not always so easy-going. Sometimes their patience ran out. Arnold's father did at least one spell in Stafford Prison, during which the family income was earned by the older boys.

When Arnold was not at school he was usually out trying to earn a few coppers. He mucked out a horse; he ran errands; on Saturdays, until ten o'clock at night, he watched over the outside display of a draper's shop and took the money for small purchases. All this standing and walking about was a trouble to Arnold because of his Bad Foot. This deserves capitalisation because it was an institution. Arnold's Bad Foot was the central fact of his boyhood. He suffered from a skin disease called grimly, Lupus: a disease, probably related to tuberculosis, which produces suppurating patches of rawness. It is the kind of disease that only attacks people who live the kind of life Arnold had to live, and consequently is very rare in the England of today. He had two patches of it, one on the inside of his right arm just above the elbow, and the other on the upper part of his right foot. The arm was easier to bear than the foot, which had to be crushed into a hard boot every morning, to the accompaniment of tears of pain. Nobody in the household, of course, ever suggested sandals. They had never seen a pair of sandals, and would in any case not have wanted Arnold making a spectacle of himself.

Equally obviously, Arnold's parents never took him to a

doctor because they could not have paid the bill. Medical provision for the poor in those days was mainly a matter of going to hospital, and this Arnold would never have done as long as his feet, however diseased, could enable him to run away and hide. If he had heard bad stories about school, he had heard utterly terrifying ones about the things they did to you in hospital.

The only approach to medical care he ever had was an occasional visit to a woman called Nurse Mellor, who dispensed very simple treatments from her little house. Nurse Mellor would bravely tackle almost anything that was wrong with you, knowing that if she did not there was no one else who would. She would put on poultices, mix lotions and medicines, even extract teeth – though she had of course no means of giving anaesthetics, and the tooth sometimes took quite a time to dig out. Nurse Mellor's compassionate heart was touched when skinny little Arnold used to roll up his sleeve and show her the patch of lupus on his arm. 'My poor boy,' she would murmur as she applied some simple and not very effective medicament. He never showed her his foot.

Is all this harrowing? Gentle reader, be comforted. The story of Arnold is about to take on a more cheerful tone.

The misery of his foot, and his low health in general, obviously spoilt his childhood; but they were, in all probability, the reason why he survived to live into old age. When Arnold was twenty, the 1914–18 war broke out. Since he was of military age from the very beginning, and would presumably have been in the Infantry, the chances of his living through until November 1918 would have been very small. Physical standards for recruitment were low; you had to have something really wrong with you, something as serious as Arnold's lupus, to be turned down. Arnold was turned down. For the next few years the general unfairness of life, which up to that point had worked against him, came into operation in his favour. Arnold was wretchedly educated, but he was quick and adaptable, eager to seize his chances and rise above his pitiful beginnings; and with virtually all the men of his generation away, many of them never to return, opportunities were plentiful. He entered gainful employment; with better food, his health improved; his lupus at last received some competent attention in a hospital. Life became something more than a continual struggle against hunger, pain and humiliation. Arnold at twenty-one resembled a young cherry-tree which, at first stunted by bitter winds, has begun to blossom. He went on putting out blossoms until death came to him sixty years later.

Fundamental decisions were made in quick succession, for Arnold was a young cherry-tree in a hurry. One Bank Holiday he and a friend – this was in one of the last of those long, peaceful summers before the world crashed – went out for the day to Rudyard Lake. This, an artificial lake serving as a reservoir for the Potteries, lies in picturesque country, and in those days before the petrol engine was common it was the favourite day out for young people from those towns. You took the tram as far as it went and then walked, the last couple of miles being along Dunwood Lane, a small pretty road clinging to the edge of a tree-lined ridge. It was a great place for romantic encounters; many people in middle life had sentimental memories of summer outings to Rudyard Lake. Mr and Mrs Kipling even named their son after it.

On this Bank Holiday, Arnold and his friend were walking along Dunwood Lane when they noticed two girls, also in Bank Holiday clothes and Bank Holiday mood, coming towards them. In a moment of bravado, they dared each other to go up to these girls and begin a conversation. After that, there could be no backing down, and the four ended by walking back to the town together. Arnold found himself talking to the one with brown eyes and long clustering dark hair, almost gipsy-like, shy and (he felt) mysterious. With some difficulty, he got out of her who she was and where she lived. She had a sweetheart, but within a year or so the sweetheart went to the trenches and the trenches opened and swallowed him for ever. Arnold pressed on with his courtship; she consented; they became man and wife.

As Arnold's life emerged into something like the sunshine – much more like it, at any rate, than anything in the crepuscular years of his boyhood – so the basic diagram of his personality began to emerge for bystanders to see. People who are deprived and humilated in childhood nearly always go one of two ways. Either they grow up shy and diffident, asking only to creep through life as inconspicuously as possible, or they react into bumptiousness. Arnold does not quite fit this usual categorisation because he was never bumptious. He had a vein of humour and a sense of proportion which effectively guarded him against that fate. On the other hand he was certainly not shy. His lack of a decent education, his unawareness of anything that went on outside the life of his own neighbourhood, his unimpressive physique – none of these, not all of these together, inhibited him from a general willingness to participate, to have a go, to involve himself in any kind of situation and generally to take the stage. He had a natural gift for public speaking; he could sometimes be tongue-tied in the presence of individuals, if he found them grand or daunting, but he was never tongue-tied before a crowd.

During his growing-up years, the family had been entirely lacking in any sense of unity, of the shared experience of life. Arnold could never recall any one of them asking any other one where he or she had been that day, or what doing. You came in and went out, engrossed in your own purposes, and the miserable little house seemed an abode of strangers, without even the down-and-out companionship of a doss-house. Instead of being conditioned by this into accepting invisibility and wanting to blend more and more closely into his background, Arnold reacted into a fierce need for attention. If his temperament and his circumstances had been different, he might have become a politician, of the kind who rises into politics by way of street-corner meetings and soap-box oratory. Instead, the path that opened before him was that of religion.

Yes, religion. The early years of this century saw a great deal of evangelising among the poor. The legacy of Victorian industrialism – slums, ignorance, densely crowded streets where the people had lost all memory of their centuries of village life – created a need which the Church of England, busy ministering to the middle class in their stiff collars and Sunday hats, was not equipped to meet. To some extent the Nonconformist churches met this need, but even they did not often get down to the level of the hard industrial working classes, let alone the drunks and derelicts who were the concern of General Booth's Salvation Army.

The Church of England did its best in a worried, paternalistic, amateurish way. In particular it established the Church Army – a straight copy of the Salvation Army, with uniforms, ranks, bands, open-air meetings – and it set up Missions, humble brick halls where people might feel at home whose clothes were too shabby, and whose manners too unceremonious, for the solemnity of a parish church.

The Church Army used to hold open-air meetings, singing hymns, saying prayers, shouting the gospel message to passers-by, Salvationist style, and at these meetings people of every kind would 'testify'. Sometimes a reformed drunkard would stand up and tell his neighbours that the Lord Jesus had helped him to leave drink alone. Sometimes it would even be a child who spoke up. One evening, when Arnold was about twelve, the Church Army captain invited him to stand on a chair, out there on the pavement, and speak of his religious connections and emotions to the ring of upturned faces about him.

What were these convictions, these emotions? I have no doubt that they were genuine enough. The religious animal and the political animal are, obviously, not totally distinct species; they can interbreed, and produce a mixture within the same individual. There have been many examples on the Catholic Right, especially in France, of a political career fuelled by religious attitudes; and, especially in England, of the 'nonconformist conscience' impelling men and women into Labour politics in cases where the actual belief in God has not survived childhood. And yet Arnold does not quite fit that pattern

either. He was too earthy, too vividly responsive to the things of
this world, to belong to the category of the naturally religious,
though he undoubtedly had other-worldly feelings and intui-
tions. He was too impatient with intrigue, too little interested in
power, to be a true political animal, though he undoubtedly felt
impatience at evil and muddle and suffering. He was on some
kind of middle ground of his own. Perhaps, given the appropriate background, he might have been an actor (he was, in fact, a
dab hand at amateur theatricals). One thing is certain: the
neglect, the indifference, the loneliness of growing up at the
bottom of the social heap and at the bottom of the family heap in
that comfortless little house left him with a fierce need for
attention. By the time he was about sixteen, he was clear in his
own mind – whether he actually expressed it in those terms or,
more probably, not – that what he wanted most was for people
to look at him and listen to him.

The avenue to this lay through the Church. In adolescence,
Arnold's ambition was to be a Church Army captain. When
other career prospects opened up to him, and when his young
wife began to bring him a family, this notion was discarded, but
the Church remained the channel through which his energies
could flow. He passed the simple examination necessary to
become a Lay Reader, empowered to conduct services (except
for pronouncing the Blessing), and deliver sermons. His
preaching was fiery and eloquent. He spoke from a few notes,
improvising round his central statements as the best speakers in
every field have always done simply because there is no other
way. From that first childish 'testimony' piped out while
standing on a chair, he progressed to sermons which filled the
churches, all over North Staffordshire, to which he was invited.
He was always in demand; many a hard-worked parson, longing for a Sunday evening to himself for once, felt the relief of
being able to depend on Arnold to turn up and give an
electrifying sermon. He might not have welcomed Arnold as an
ordained cleric in a neighbouring parish, offering week-by-
week competition to his own more pedestrian style; but as an

occasional performer Arnold was perfect. Or, at any rate, near enough to perfection for the then Archdeacon of Stoke (it had duly become a federated City since Arnold's birth) to offer him what amounted to a cure of souls.

I have said that the Church of England struggled to keep up in the evangelical field by two means, the Church Army and the Mission. One such mission stood on a brick-strewn piece of waste ground near the canal which led from Stoke to Trent Vale and outward. The name of this stretch, this non-place, was 'Potts's Ground'; correctly, I suppose, it should have been pronounced 'Pottses,' but the populace, and Arnold with them, never called it anything but 'Pot's Ground,' as if some enormous pot had cleared a space round itself – which, in larger terms, was just about what *had* happened.

Potts's Ground was in Boothen, and was officially a subsidiary or satellite of All Saints' Church, Boothen, a pleasant and unpretentious Victorian church, now demolished, as the canal has been filled in and Potts's Ground itself obliterated by the restless tide of city development. All Saints' Church may have been unpretentious, but it was awesome enough for the people in the poorer quarters to avoid it. Potts's Ground Mission was where they worshipped, or nowhere. And now, some time in the mid 1920s, the Archdeacon invited Arnold to take over the running of the Mission.

Officially this involved holding a service every Sunday night, with Church of England hymns and prayers and a sermon. There was a choir, selected from among the congregation, who sang the hymns from the platform, but the composition of this choir depended more on strategic than musical considerations. A backslider, who appeared at the Sunday evening service three weeks running and then stayed away for four or five, would be more likely to be invited to join the choir than someone with a good voice who reliably attended week after week. Why not? The reliable worshipper with the good voice would be singing anyway. By such harmless arts, but most of all by the eloquence of his preaching, Arnold filled Potts's Ground Mission and kept

it full for seven years, at the end of which even his vitality began
to run out. For the running of the Mission was not something
that occupied Sunday only. These people, rough, untaught,
working for low wages, needed a spiritual guide and, amazingly, they accepted Arnold in this role. I say 'amazingly' because
people are usually reluctant to concede any authority to someone they have always known. And in Arnold's case it was not
merely that they had always known him. He had started life
among them, which is usually enough on its own to provoke the
'We-knew-him-when' reaction, and what a start! His birthplace
was scarcely a mile from Potts's Ground, and what a birthplace!
These people had seen Arnold as a half-starved, ragged child;
they knew the slum he came from; they had seen his father
shambled home from the pub and doubtless some of them had
seen him being led away by policemen for not paying the rent.
Arnold came among them not only with none of the advantages
of the stranger from an unknown background who can be made
the object of interesting speculation; not even with the reason-
able head-start of being from a family that was respected in the
town; he started right back, from the most handicapped position, and by the sheer force of his personality, his energy, his
kindliness, his unstinted commitment, he gained authority, an
authority which held good right to the gates of death. When
people in the Potts's Ground district were dying – and in those
days people mostly died at home rather than in hospital –
Arnold would be sent for. Still young, still skinny and unimpressive, but known, trusted and admired, he sat by many a
death-bed, fanning some fevered sufferer with a newspaper and
saying the last prayers.

Arnold never gave up the pulpit. It was too deeply in his
blood. To say what he had to say within a context of religious
ritual, amid hymn-singing and prayer-murmuring, appealed to
something very central in him. On the other hand his sermons
usually had some social content. His message was always,
intellectually, a simple one: deny yourself, put other people
first, forgive your enemies, and do these things within the

context of the society you live in. As he gained in age and authority, he expanded his activities into the field of local politics. He became a City Councillor and a magistrate.

During the Second World War, when (at any rate after 1941) popular enthusiasm for the Soviet Union mounted to a great height, Arnold shared this enthusiasm to the full. He made the assumption, as many people did, that the war-time alliance would make a foundation for lasting friendship and co-operation, that the mutual suspicion of the years since 1917 would be forgotten. He worked tirelessly for his local area of Anglo-Soviet friendship, finally joining the platform at a mass meeting in the city's biggest hall some time in 1942. The other speakers, who were all professional politicians, seemed poor speakers by comparison with Arnold. They were avuncular, or rambling, or self-indulgent, or emptily rabble-rousing, or all by turns. He spoke briefly, lucidly, forcefully. The performance did not go unremarked. In the course of the next three or four years it was several times suggested to him that he should stand for Parliament. The suggestion, I gather, was a serious one, made by various MPs, who stood ready to set the necessary arrangements in motion; and with Arnold's local support he could scarcely have failed to win a seat. He pondered; hesitated; finally decided, wisely, to remain a big fish in a small pond. The size and complexity of Westminster were, understandably, frightening to the boy from Johnson's Terrace and Cross Street School, however far he had come and however much he had grown. The loss to the world was not great; the gain to his own neighbourhood, appreciable.

When Arnold had an important speech to prepare, such as the one with which he dominated that Anglo-Soviet meeting, it was his practice (except in the dead of winter) to get up at about 5 a.m., drive his car out into the country and think out his speech amid the silence and freshness he found there. Stoke-on-Trent, even after thirty years of expansion, is still not a large city, though a quarter of a million people live there; in those days it was smaller, and very attractive countryside came close

on all sides. Arnold loved this countryside. He knew the wide
moorlands to the north, the gentle dairy-farming country to the
west and south; even the more flat and featureless stretch to the
east, towards Derby and Nottingham, had some charms for
him. He was a lifelong walker, at home where there were trees
and grass and open views. And this was one of the two causes of
the close companionship we enjoyed for so many years. I shared
his taste for country walks and was impressed by his local
knowledge – he knew the prettiest villages and the quietest
footpaths – and also by his unusually developed sense of
direction, a quality I totally lack. Sometimes we would walk in
the high stone-wall country towards Buxton – the southern
fringe, really, of the Peak District – and he would park the car
on a long lonely road without obvious landmarks, strike off
across what to me was a trackless moor, describe a wide circle
for three or four hours, and come back to within fifty yards of
the car. He was a good walking companion, and I too had
something to contribute to these excursions because I have
always been a good listener. Talking out his ideas as his legs
moved steadily onward was not just something he did in
isolation; he was just as ready to do it with a companion. I have
walked over scores of miles, in all kinds of weather, to the sound
of Arnold's voice as he developed and, I think, clarified for
himself his views on politics, on social issues, on religion. I like
to think that that was something I did for him. Another thing I
did was to introduce him, in late middle life, to the pleasure of
drinking beer in country pubs. I had to overcome a resistance
here, because his early experiences had left him, understandably, with the idea that the door of a public house was the road
to ruin; but once I accustomed him to it he enjoyed chatting
with the other customers, and to stop at a pub became a part of
his pattern of country walks, as it always had been of mine. I
dwell on the trivial matter because in our long relationship he
influenced me greatly, and I influenced him, except in this one
small custom, not at all.

    Arnold loved the countryside, he loved people and bustle, he

loved the cut and thrust of debate and the drama of holding an
audience. And so on. He was the furthest removed from those
people who yawn in the face of creation and declare themselves
'bored'. To him, life was continuously interesting and exciting
– which is not, of course, to say that he found it continuously
pleasant. He had his sufferings, his annoyances, and frustra-
tions, like anyone else. But he was, as any truly vital person is,
spared the dusty corridor of boredom. If I had to choose one
word to fit Arnold, I think that word would be *responsive*.

It was always marvellous to see, as a prime example, how
vividly he responded to women. Put him in front of a woman, or
a knot of women, whom he found in the slightest degree
attractive, and his face, his eyes, his whole body took on an
intense alertness. I don't know whether Arnold was, in practical
terms, much of a womaniser; the issue does not much concern
me; doubtless it would be unrealistic to expect someone as
tuned-in to women as he was to go through a long life without
having his little adventures along the way. What does concern
me, because I so often marvelled at it, was how the magnetic
feminine principle drew that wonderful energy to the surface in
him.

In the summer of 1975 a play of mine was put on at the
Victoria Theatre, Stoke-on-Trent. Arnold, then eighty years
old, came to the first night; the performance was followed by a
party for the cast and friends, and I shall never forget the sight
of Arnold at this party, holding forth to a semi-circle of young
actresses whose prettiness seemed to come more vividly to life
because of his obvious appreciation of it. Fun, enjoyment,
gaiety, radiated from his frail old body.

And frail, by that time, it was in truth. That summer, which
was long and sun-baked, he enjoyed to the full, sitting in his
garden or strolling in the countryside. With the first cold touch
of autumn he developed a bad chill, and suddenly, as happens
with very old people, everything went wrong at once. Through
the winter he lay at death's door, but (whether mercifully or
not) very sophisticated medical treatment kept him alive, and

with the first sun of spring he somehow struggled into his clothes and even went out. 'I shall be better when the good weather comes,' he told me; and in this faith we went for a walk together one April day. It was a ghostly memory of his old, striding walks; I drove him into the countryside, we got out of the car and, standing on a knob of rising ground, plotted a triangular promenade of about a mile.

Long before the mile was covered, Arnold was wilting. There simply was no strength left in that old body which had weathered malnutrition and disease seventy years earlier and had gone on at a cracking pace ever since. We walked more and more slowly. I was about to suggest he sit down while I fetched the car when we heard behind us the drumming engine of a tractor. It came up, towing behind a flat wagon which had been emptied of its load. We flagged it down. The driver, a good-natured young fellow, let us scramble up on to the wagon, and sitting on its smooth boards, dusty with fragments of straw and chaff, we finished our triangle. Arnold looked round with satisfaction at the slowly-moving landscape, and remarked that this would be a good way of taking a holiday; touring the British Isles by tractor and trailer.

That was the last of my excursions with Arnold. His bed, and then the grave, claimed him in the first height of summer, the time of year he loved so much, and his life ended among springing green leaves and clamorous birds. But I remember him jolting along behind the tractor, enjoying the fun of it, finding zest in that last outing as he had found zest in all the others.

I was very proud of Arnold. He was my father.

At Tantine's

IN THE MORNINGS the valley lay in deep shadow and the air was thin and cold. You could hear the hurrying of the little river that ran down from the foot of the massif, the sounds carrying all the way across the valley in the still air. The stream was hidden from the eye under its roof of mist, but the racing cold-water sound made you imagine the smooth bubbles, the swirl of the water over jutting rocks, the dark frozen mud and the crusted bead-patterns of ice along the margins. If you wanted to know whether the valley would be warm and bright with sunshine that day, it was no use looking at the sky, because its porcelain grey gave no real indication of what was to come. The trick was to wait until the sun peeped over the jagged rim of the massif and sent a few rays shooting out horizontally, then to turn round and look the opposite way. The valley had the shape of a bath-tub, one end knocked out; if you looked at the distance beyond the open end you saw a range of very tall peaks (the Dents du Midi?), and if the day was going to be sunny the first rays would light up the two or three highest of them. Every day began in the same way: open the windows, fold back the green wooden shutters, step out on to the balcony with its fringe of icicles; shiver a little, look to the left till the sun edged over, look to the right to see whether the peaks were shining or stayed misty purple; and make the day's plans accordingly.

In the weeks before the smow came, the time of waiting between summer and winter, the floor of the valley would be warm and sunny until about two-thirty in the afternoon, and then the tide of shadow would begin to move up the slopes. By about four the village as a whole would have entered evening, but the scattered chalets higher up would have sun for a while yet, and the really high ones, clinging to the furthest open ground just below the timber-line, would have dazzling window-panes and sun-warmed wood until Dr Daniel had made his last visit and it was time for him to start up the Vespa's little popping motor, and we would begin to move down the long, steep tracks with their ruts and loose stones. Sitting behind him I could feel the fat little tyres grabbing for a hold in the gravel, bouncing in and out of the wheel-ruts, bumping over the larger stones. The pillion seat had a looped handle at the front and I would hang on to this as we went down, down, down, like an aircraft, into the dark lake of shadow.

One evening Hans Mathyse came into the Pension with a fox he had shot. He laid the body, already stiffening, down on the bench just inside the entrance and went into the bar for a drink. I heard them greeting him and laughing. Everybody liked Hans, as I did myself. I was going to follow him into the bar but something halted me and I stood for a moment looking down at the body of the fox. The coat was a beautiful rich red, with pure white underneath. It was a bigger animal than an English fox. In England its size would have meant that it must be a male, but on the Alpine slopes a vixen might grow to that size. Without examining the appropriate parts I could not be sure whether it was male or female, and I felt that beautiful dead wild creature deserved better than to be prodded. If it was a vixen would she have been foraging for cubs? And would the cubs starve now that she was dead?

Hans Mathyse was as brave as a wild animal, and as strong, and as patient, and as wise in the ways of the weather and the earth. The fox had been out in search of prey, and Hans Mathyse had been out in search of prey. I don't think he actually 'went hunting', he left that to the city people at weekends, but it would be second nature to him to have his gun ready and to shoot anything bigger than a squirrel. It was what men like him had always done. He could not eat the fox, but he could get a few francs for its head and its brush; some tourist-trap of a café would mount them on the wall, or they would go into the 'games room' at someone's holiday chalet. His shooting the fox was exactly the same as the fox pouncing on a rabbit.

One day it would be the turn of Hans Mathyse to be killed, by an avalanche, or a falling tree, or perhaps by a bacillus or a blood-clot, and he would meet death as bravely and defiantly as the fox. Both were mountain creatures and nothing had softened them. In that respect they were friends and comrades.

Monsieur Armand and Monsieur Paul were sitting outside the Pension after their lunch in the warm spring sunlight, drinking coffee. Their hard peaked caps, black with a white band, were lying beside them on the circular metal tables, their middle-aged faces were pink with the strong sun and they looked very contented. They greeted me as I went out.

I was not going far. In those days I used to like to eat chocolate after lunch and I had run out. I was going to the shop just down the street, at the junction of the small road that ran into the village of Les Diablerets and the even smaller road that went up the mountain and over the Col des Mosses. I would hesitate before the not very large display among the miscellaneous groceries and try to make up my mind which kind of chocolate took my fancy just then: nuts, no nuts, milk, plain, or Toblerone with honey and almonds. Sometimes I chose that white chocolate, very sweet and milky, because at twenty-nine I had not quite sloughed off all the tastes of my childhood. To eat that stuff was as childish as spooning up sweetened condensed milk out of a tin, but my tastes were consistently adult only nineteen days out of twenty, and this might be the twentieth.

It would not take me long to choose the chocolate and pay for it, and then I was going to go back into the Pension, climb the stairs, go into my room and come out on to the balcony above the tables where Monsieur Paul and Monsieur Armand were sitting, and then I too would sit in the early afternoon sun. I would eat squares of chocolate and look round at the quiet village street, trodden snow underfoot, crisp snow on the roofs, and hear the steady drip-drip of the thaw as the icicles shortened. In the sharp February night they would lengthen again, and in the warm still hours in the middle of the day they would shorten once more, and that was the springtime in its beginning

phase. Its later phase was slush, and the sudden sliding of acres
of snow from the hillsides, exposing raw brown earth from
which the grass had died back during the long white winter, and
rapid brooks running faster and faster as their jagged canopies
of ice melted and swelled the channels of racing water they had
so deeply hidden from sight all winter long. Its last phase, just
before full summer, was rich new grass and mountain slopes
blue with gentians, but I had never seen that.

Whatever choice of chocolate I made, I should be coming
back in about five minutes, but the chances were that Monsieur
Paul and Monsieur Armand would be gone by then, walking
down the road to the station to take the afternoon train down. It
went at five minutes past two. They worked for the Aigle–
Sépéy–Diablerets railway. I believe Monsieur Armand was a
driver and Monsieur Paul was the guard and ticket-collector,
though I also have the impression that on that small mountain
railway everybody did everything. At any rate, Monsieur Paul
and Monsieur Armand used to come to the Pension at such
times as were dictated by their work. If they were on the
ordinary day-time run, they got to the terminus as Les
Diablerets at twelve noon. They had lunch at the Pension and
went down the mountain again at five past two. If they were on
the last run up in the evening, which got there at about ten
o'clock, they stayed the night at the Pension and took the
morning train at a quarter to seven.

The Pension was Tantine's. It was called 'Les Lilas'. Monsieur Paul and Monsieur Armand were not the only railway men
who used it, but they are the ones I remember. They had a
status that was not quite the same as that of ordinary guests in
the Pension, such as myself. They did not take their meals in
the restaurant but in the bar, and at night they slept in small
rooms at the back of the house. In fact, their position was higher
than ours. They were regulars, we were transients. Even a
pensionnaire like myself, spending a whole autumn and winter
at Les Lilas, was a transient compared with Monsieur Paul and
Monsieur Armand.

If you were a friend of Tantine's you were in at Les Lilas; in like Flynn, as we used to say in those days when Errol cut such a swath across the world. Tantine owned the Pension, the Pension owned her, it was her world and her realm, she never went anywhere else, and if she liked you the house liked you too. It was just a simple wooden chalet, and Tantine herself was just a little old woman in a black dress, but together they made a world.

Tantine had always run Les Lilas. At least, if there was a time when she had done anything else, one never heard about it. And her frugal habits, her anxious attention to business, obviously dated back to a period when trade had been nothing like so good as it was now, in the rising 'fifties. She had run the place with her unmarried brother. By all accounts, it was the old story of a brother with plenty of suavity and charm, showing a bonhomous face to the world, not very convinced of the virtues of hard work as long as he could get his needs attended to without it, and a sister not endowed with fine plumage who devotedly slaved in the background. Tantine, in short, did the work while her brother provided excellent company in the bar and thus, to be fair, was probably good for business in his own way.

Business must have needed looking after because, first, there was the gradual decline of Les Diablerets as a resort, which resulted, I imagine, from that increasing cult of the sun which grew up in the inter-war years. The village lost ground to its rivals because it lay so deep down on the floor of the bathtub, and on short winter days it had barely four or five hours of sun, which was fine for the Edwardians but not for the new heliotropic generations. (When German doctors, trying to combat the effects of the British blockade in 1919, discovered that sunlight could help to overcome certain vitamin deficiencies in children, they unleashed on the world a vogue that had unforeseeable consequences.) The second blow to fall was the 1939–45 War, which put a stop to tourism. There had been years when she had had to sink her pride and go out and tout for any stray bit of business; at weekends she used to stand beside the road at the entrance to the village, just where cars have to slow down, and stop the drivers and ask them if they wanted anywhere to stay for the night. (Notice that it was Tantine who did this, not the brother.)

After the war, when Switzerland was just about the only country in Europe in any shape to receive tourists, trade must have picked up fairly quickly. Tantine's brother, though, did not live long enough to enjoy this new comfort; he was killed in a car accident in about 1951. Two friends who were with him also died. The three of them are buried in one grave beside the picturesque old Protestant church at Vers L'Eglise, and the long tombstone, bordering all three of their heads, shows the outline of the *massif* of Les Diablerets. With his death, Tantine entered something like widowhood. I did not know her before it happened, to form a direct comparison, but there was something widow-like in the black dress she invariably wore and in the resignation that showed in her face when it was in repose.

It was not, by any means, always in repose. Tantine was an outgoing woman with plenty of character. She had a temper; when she let it loose (generally on some member of the workforce or on a younger relative) you could hear her all over the house. And she, beyond all doubt, knew the softer emotions of love.

In particular, Tantine loved Monsieur Armand. I think it was his gentleness that won her heart. Monsieur Paul was a more lively character with a touch of devilment, not above snatching a kiss from a fair fellow-lodger if he could get away with it. Monsieur Armand seemed to radiate both the innocence of a child and the gentleness of some patient animal such as the ox. Indeed his broad face, with its large eyes, was rather bovine in a handsome way. When Tantine was sitting with Monsieur Armand, snatching one of her brief intervals of leisure (she never sat down for long), she looked at him so tenderly, and her smile was of such indescribable sweetness, that one realised all over again the power of love to make a woman beautiful.

I was at Les Lilas because I was hiding from the world. For the last two or three years my life had been heavily weighted with what appeared to me insoluble problems – they were, in the end, solved only by the sort of action that one dreads to embark on; divorce, the selling-up of a home, a series of traumatic breaks and difficult new beginnings – and my physical health, reflecting the narrowness and gloom of my inward life, had been cracking. The one positive thing I had been doing was to write, desultorily, in fits and starts, my novel *Hurry On Down*. I started this as early as 1949, and added a few pages to it now and again, with no very high hopes of its ever seeing the light; but in 1952, realising that I must finally finish or abandon it, I worked steadily at it throughout the summer, a dreadful summer of emotional difficulties for me. It was finished by the time the University term began in the autumn of 1952, and in the next few weeks it found a publisher and began, independently now of me, its journey towards the light.

In the summer of 1953 I was ill again and in hospital for an operation. When I came out I knew I had to get myself together somehow. I made arrangements to take a year off work, during which I planned to support myself by writing, and in early October I left England, intending to go first to the Swiss Alps and then consider the next moves as my strength began to return.

I left England at the very time when *Hurry On Down* was published – perhaps on the actual day. While my book was being reviewed and discussed and my fate as a writer decided, I was a long way off and a lot higher up, hidden from the world by fold after fold of mountains, sinking peacefully into the world of Les Lilas, into Tantine's world.

When, in that summer of 1953, I told people I was going to drop out of the scene for a few months and go off in search of rest and health, there were worldly-wise shakings of head among those of my acquaintances who constitutionally Knew Best. To take a rest was all right, but my choice of place was wrong. Why Switzerland? I'd be bored. It was such a boring little country.

Bored, boring, boredom, the words rang through their admonitions till I wonder why I wasn't frightened off. One, a seasoned old campaigner who had been around for ever and known everybody, made a counter-suggestion. He knew of a place in Sweden that he was sure would suit me. He could furnish information and introductions – I had only to say the word. I thought about it for a week, then thanked him and declined the offer. What profound instinct guided me I shall never know, but I shall always be grateful to it. Without having the materials for a wise decision, I nevertheless made one.

For I was not bored in Switzerland. To begin with – and this is going to sound a trifle priggish – I do not happen to have the temperament that *can* be bored in the presence of the most sublime and magnificent works of Nature. And then again, without disrespect to my Scandinavian friends, 'Europe' as a concept is much more interesting than 'Scandinavia' as a concept. And Switzerland is, above all things, European. Tiny country as it is, with one community traditionally divided from the next by almost impassable mountains, it is in the middle of Western Europe, right in the path of everyone's comings and goings. During the first months at Tantine's, the autumn months, I was the only foreigner in the valley. But once the winter holiday season started and it began to fill up, it filled up with French, with Italians, with Germans, with English even. The nearest town of any size, Lausanne, is very solidly Swiss, but a few miles further on down the line was Geneva, one of the biggest international communities in the world.

For me, that winter in Switzerland came just in time: just in time, that is, to make a European of me before my mind set firmly in a narrow national mould. I was, at twenty-eight, remarkably ignorant. I had been wretchedly educated up to University level, and at the University the subject-matter of my education had been entirely English. Even my smattering of schoolroom French had begun to fade. Now, and suddenly, I had to dig out those odds and ends of French and get them working. If I wanted the news, I got it from Radio Suisse

Romande or the *Tribune de Genève*. And unless I wanted to remain silent from morning to night, I had to use my French in conversation – with Tantine, with Monsieur Paul and Monsieur Armand, and Hans Mathyse, and Daniel the young doctor.

Tantine's heart moved with love towards the gentle Monsieur Armand; Monsieur Paul was more on my humdrum level. We used to have great jokes together. When I returned to Les Diablerets after a year's absence, and got off the express train and came out of the station at Aigle, he happened to be in the cab of the waiting Aigle–Sépéy–Diablerets train, and greeted me with a piercing toot on the whistle. I liked that. It was like being piped over the side of a ship by the bo'sun. And, though giving a toot on a train whistle hardly counts as a flamboyant gesture, it is flamboyant by the standards of the contained, impassive Swiss.

The Swiss, of course, are contained and impassive because their character has been formed by the Alps. Only one-third of Swiss soil is arable; the rest is rock and ice. Necessarily, then, a lot of this rock and ice has found its way into the human nature of the inhabitants. This may cease to be true, or become less true, as modern technological civilisation makes the life even of the *montagnard* softer and easier. To sit watching television in a double-glazed house with full central heating is not the same thing as splitting logs for the stove or breaking the ice on the water-jug in the morning, and where the horse-drawn *diligence* (aptly named!) used to take six hours to crawl from Aigle up to Les Diablerets, a car will now do it in forty-five minutes. But the sternness and stubbornness of the mountain temperament will take a few generations to breed out yet.

It so happens that I came into contact, during that autumn of 1953, with just about the last survivors of the old mountain way of life. It happened through Dr Daniel. The village doctor, who spent the winter setting the limbs of people who had injured themselves on skis and the summer setting the limbs of people

who had injured themselves in climbing accidents, took his
annual holiday in the autumn, and Daniel, a young intern
from Lausanne, was his *locum tenens*. The few people who
formed the doctor's permanent case-load were mostly geriat-
rics. Or, to drop the hideous contemporary jargon, they were
aged men and women who, having done this life's work faithful-
ly and well, were now in the process of dying, taking their time
about it if possible, in their remote chalets high up near the
timber-line. Dr Daniel used to pop-pop round the mountain
tracks on his Vespa, with his medical bag on the platform
between his feet, and with me clinging on behind. Arriving at
some ancient chalet of dark wood – the pious inscriptions of the
original owners were usually dated in the eighteenth century
and sometimes in the seventeenth – he would introduce me as
'un médecin anglais' to disarm natural suspicion of this silent,
gazing stranger, and we would enter. I shall never forget those
interiors. They were quite unlike anything one sees in a modern
home, be that home rich or poor. The ancient, dark, undecor-
ated wood, the ancestral furniture, the strings of onions and
flitches of bacon hanging on the walls . . . did they have electric
lights, or oil-lamps? I can't remember; we did our rounds in the
afternoon, when the bright autumn sun was coming in at the
window. One feature was unchanging; there was always a bed,
and in the bed there was always an old *montagnard*, male or
female, engaged in dying. I knew that I was looking at a way of
life that was passing, had already all but passed, from the earth.
In another few weeks or months, the one partner would be
dead, and the other would be tidied away into some home for
the aged, and the chalet would be stripped and modernised and
let to a city family looking for a holiday house: or else simply
allowed to fall down. Staring, wondering, I knew that I was looking at the last flicker of a tradition going back to the Middle Ages.

I also knew that I had arrived on the Diablerets scene just as the
last vestiges of that tradition were about to disappear for ever.
The village, under the leadership of a determined *Syndicat*

d'Initiative, was just beginning its long haul back to favour as a holiday resort. The white-elephant Grand Hotel, so much a drag on their resources, was mysteriously burnt to the ground a year or two later; the insurance paid up; a glittering new edifice, as modern in design as the old one was Victorian, went up in its place. The télésiège, which was being constructed in my first autumn and on which I must have been one of the first dozen or so people to ride, after the mayor and notabilities, carried visitors up to the heights of Isenau so that they could bask in winter sunshine while the bath-tub below was in near darkness; a new skating-rink, new ski-lifts, everything happened at once. But this was no mere restoration of Les Diablerets to what the place had been like in 1905. History does not stand still. The Edwardian tourist liked a combination of comfort with quiet and dignity amid the sublimities of the landscape. Modern holiday-makers like noise, colour and movement: noise especially. I have been back to Les Diablerets in recent years, the late 'seventies and early 'eighties, but not to stay long. The things I was looking for, the things I found in such glorious abundance back in 1953, have gone. Now the place is a vast playground; not even the longest walk can take one clear of the sound of the canned music blasting out from the skating-rink; pine-clad slopes that used to be wrapped in an eternal meditative silence, with the snow an untouched white sheet on which one might write one's life all over again from a new beginning, and the tall dark trunks as straight and dignified as the pillars of a cathedral, are now pestered with the whirr and clack of ski-lifts, distributed so that you are not quite out of earshot of one before you begin to hear the next. The mountain silence is fled, to return only in the winter night when the only creatures to inhabit it are the owl and the fox.

Nowadays, if I find myself in that neighbourhood, I avoid Les Diablerets itself and stop short at Vers L'Eglise, which still has its ancient rustic dignity and leaves the tourists to be catered for by its railway-bred neighbour. But even in Vers L'Eglise I do not go into the churchyard as at one time I never failed to do.

The 'rude forefathers of the hamlet' lie there, people like the ones I saw during their last days and hours on earth, and their parents and their parents' parents. So does Tantine's brother, with his two friends, under their fine headstone of the massif, three more victims of the motor car in its implacable war against the human race. And before I stopped going there, I had begun to notice new headstones with names that had been familiar to me in life. Hans Mathyse was the last new one I saw. Brave and hardy as a mountain animal, the hunter had claimed him at last, for nobody and nothing is indestructible.

Perhaps, by this time, Tantine has joined him there. And that is the real reason why I keep away from the churchyard at Vers L'Eglise. Sooner or later, Tantine will die, and her world will go with her. But I don't want to know the moment when it happens.

*The Incidental Thoughts
Of Marshall McLuhan*

MARSHALL at the wheel of his car, driving through the busy streets of Toronto with a nervous impatience that expressed itself in rapid changes of pace, now jamming the brakes full on, now trampling on the accelerator so that the car sprang forward like a greyhound that sees the electric hare receding in the distance . . . Marshall coming in out of the night in Brooklyn Heights, masculine and companionable, a cigar fuming at the corner of his mouth and that burly Irish priest in tow . . . Marshall sitting on a bar stool in Washington DC, burping with indigestion, discussing with one of the local habitués various remedies for 'gas on the stomach' . . . and always Marshall talking, talking, pouring out the continuous stream of notions that issued from his ceaselessly active mind like an unstoppable flow of ticker-tape. 'Incidentally, John, that was the moment when the Ivory Tower became the Control Tower', 'Incidentally, John, the view of the world as global village', 'Incidentally, John, it's no accident that after 1850 English prose becomes a p.a. system', 'Incidentally, John, some of the new material brought into the focus of poetry by Laforgue and Corbière was intentionally hilarious.' Everything seemed to be thrown off incidentally, as if to one or other side of the main thoroughfare of his thinking, but what it was incidental to I never could tell.

If you are a writer it is natural, though not inevitable, that some of your friends will be writers; and it is interesting, from time to time, to go mentally through the list and sort them into two categories: those whose work you read because you already knew them, and those whom you got to know because you read their work and found it interesting.

In the years immediately following the end of the Second World War, when American books and periodicals made their appearance again in English bookshops, I was a great reader of the New Criticism. Looking back now, the New Criticism seems to me a rather tame affair, and such controversy as it stirred up little more than a storm in a teacup. But it seemed different in those days, from about 1946 to 1950. For one thing, it flourished almost entirely within the English Departments of Universities, and one has to set it against the rather somnolent and unadventurous atmosphere of English literary studies in the preceding half-century or so. In the convention as then established on both sides of the Atlantic, what you did with literature was either to 'appreciate' it, which in practice meant writing sensitive little essays about it couched in rather consciously cadenced prose, or to do 'research' on it, which always meant the unearthing of new information. This information seemed to be valued not because anyone found it particularly interesting but because it had not been unearthed before: it was a 'contribution to knowledge', a notion which had evidently been taken over, largely unexamined, from the physical sciences. Against this the New Criticism put forward a predilection for intensive analysis, particularly with a view to enquiring by what means, precisely, the language of poetry obtained its effects. Since this kind of analysis made 'modern' poetry seem more interesting and acceptable, it was largely the channel whereby the post-Symbolist poets entered the subject-matter of academic discussion, whereas the preceding generation of scholars had reacted to modern writing mainly by shaking their heads over it.

In view of what was to come later, the victories of the New Criticism hardly seem worth much celebration. The intensive study of contemporary writing in Universities can be seen clearly, now that it is established, as not much of a benefit either to the academic world or to the practising writer, and as for the old standards of objectivity and 'research', they were at least better than the trendy nonsense that reigns now. Philology was better than linguistics. It may have been gently boring to listen to a scholar discoursing, out of a vast knowledge, about Scandinavian roots and loan-words and dialect forms, but at least the scholar *knew* something and could solve real problems; his views were more worth listening to than glib theorising about linguistics by people who can't speak or write any language but their own.

Yes, I have to work hard to think myself back into the state of mind in which the New Criticism seemed exciting and liberating, and when I do so I recall the whole atmosphere of those years, the food shortages and the skimpily produced books and the Universities full of returned warriors, the older ones anxious to get back to something called 'normality' which the younger ones, never having known it, were not certain they would recognise if they saw it; and my own early twenties.

Then it is that I remember the physical feel of those thick, well-funded periodicals, lavishly produced with good printing and wide margins, in which the New Criticism could be read. They were heaped up in tempting piles on the counters of University bookshops, Blackwell's in Oxford, Heffer's in Cambridge and the like. I suppose in publishing terms their sales in England were negligible, amounting to a few score. But they made an impact on the small world in which I had my being, a world in which poetry and criticism were what we mainly talked about. I eyed and fingered them in the shops; when I could (for they were expensive) I bought them; and when I bought a copy I read it to pieces. I can see those magazines now – the *Sewanee Review*, the *Kenyon Review*, the *Hudson Review*. They arrived like ambassadors from a world that seemed both inciting and reassuring, a world where people were interested in the same things that we were, but looked at them in a different way.

Since this essay is about Marshall McLuhan, it is obvious what I am going to say next; that in these thick, shiny reviews I first became acquainted with his name. Quite so. And yet 'Herbert Marshall McLuhan', as he tended to sign himself, was not quite the ordinary New Critic. He wrote what I used to think of as 'brain-teeming' criticism. Where the traditional scholar rarely ventured outside his 'field', and the conventional New Critic applied what were becoming well-worn techniques to the text in front of him (the sacred phrase was 'the words on the page'), McLuhan worked by sending up a shower of comparisons, analogies, wisecracks, sudden satiric jabs at people and attitudes he disliked, and equally sudden excursions into scholastic philosophy or modern advertising practice (both these last were subjects he had studied attentively), all in the service of illuminating, or preparing for illumination, whatever book or writer he was discussing. It was like riding on a roller-coaster; it also reminded me of Johnson's description of the practice of the Metaphysical poets: 'the most heterogeneous ideas are yoked by violence together.' In McLuhan's case the violence had nothing sullen or offensive about it; it was the natural outcrop of a geniality, an impatience with conventional categories, and a willingness to have a go and try anything for size. Most critics make an *aperçu* serve them as theme for a whole essay or even a whole book; McLuhan provided an *aperçu* in virtually every line, and if they were not all equally good, if indeed some of them were unconvincing to the point of absurdity, well, there was always the interest of seeing what the man would say next; and there was a large, gusty breeze of fresh air blowing through the whole enterprise.

I remember feeling more than once that if the title of any of McLuhan's essays were to get lost, no one would be able to say, from reading the essay, what it had actually been *about*. In the 1950s he began to contribute to English periodicals; I believe the first British editor to use him was Cyril Connolly, who included an essay on 'American Advertising' in the number of *Horizon*, in 1950s, that dealt specifically with the American scene. You could at any rate tell what that one was about; but when Marshall moved to the Oxford periodical *Essays in Criticism* a little later, he contributed an essay on 'Tennyson and Picturesque Poetry' (I, iii, 1951) which gave me the impression, on reading it, of having to keep my seat-belt fastened. Here is a specimen paragraph:

It might be suggested that landscape offered several attractive advantages to the poets of the mid-eighteenth century. It meant for one thing an extension of the Baroque interest in *la peinture de la pensée*, which the study of Seneca had suggested to Montaigne and Bacon and Browne – an interest which reached a maximal development, so far as the technique of direct statement permitted, in Pascal, Racine, and Alexander Pope. Pope especially deserves study from this point of view since he first developed the couplet to do the complex work of the double plot of the Elizabethans. He discovered how to make a couplet achieve a symbolic vision. That is, to effect an instant of inclusive consciousness by the *juxtaposition without copula* of diverse and even paradoxical situations or states of mind:

> The hungry judges soon the sentence sign,
> And wretches hang that jurymen may dine.

The judges are hungry but not for justice; yet there is no suggestion that they would be better judges if they had dined. The stark confrontation of this human condition is enforced by the second line or 'sub-plot' which is parallel but inferior. The suggestion that meat must hang before it is edible, and that jurymen are merely promoting the proper business of society by seeing that it gets hung is analogous to the vision of society in Swift's *Modest Proposal* and to Lear's vision on the heath. The couplet in Pope's hands escaped from the conditions imposed by univocal discourse which had developed in the Cartesian milieu.

Let no one imagine that I am quoting such a paragraph satirically, to show Marshall as a quaint or clownish figure. On the contrary, I admired it then and I admire it now. I like the sweep and audacity, the impression he gives of having so much to say about so many subjects that one thought can scarcely be brought in without three or four others which have a bearing on it, a bearing often hitherto unsuspected. The incidentals are as important as the main line, the digressions as essential as the ratiocinative thread. In that respect Marshall was very like Sterne (who had an Irish mother); and when you add his veneration for James Joyce and the fact that during the war years he had been in close contact with Wyndham Lewis, another adventurous polymath and controversialist, the lineage becomes a little clearer. It wasn't straight 'New Criticism' by any means; it was McLuhanism.

I found these essays enormously helpful in the development of my own mind, not that it was ever going to resemble his mind – we were very different types, and the friendship that developed between us was at least partly a friendship of opposites. But where the New Criticism slightly bored me, and the tradition of 'contributing to knowledge' seemed to me a dead hand, McLuhan's essays galvanised me into a new awareness of the diversity and richness of the field there was to be cultivated. I also liked his watchful, ironic eye on the social scene: no ivory-tower scholar he; his chief claim for literary study, indeed, was that it sharpened one's response to experience and helped one to stand out from what he called the 'zombie horde' of urban consumers.

When, in 1951, his first foray into social criticism appeared – *The Mechanical Bride*, a study of advertising techniques – I was ready for it. The blend of learning, speculation, satire, and comic-strip presentation seemed to me an idiom that only McLuhan could have developed; and now, thirty-odd years later, I am sure I was right. I had a great deal of trouble getting hold of a copy; it was brought out by the Vanguard Press, New York, who did not seem to have a British distributor, and it is a neat instance of the complicated web of relationships that makes up the most ordinary life that the person who ultimately lent me a copy was F.P. Wilson. That gentle, grave and learned man was Merton Professor of English Literature at Oxford during the brief time I spent in graduate study, and though I was manifestly a square peg in a round hole ('research', as Wilson and his colleagues pursued it, was not my line of country and I think it was a relief to everybody when I got that fact straight and just went away) he treated me with courtesy and kindliness, sharing with me his vast knowledge whenever I was in any kind of position to benefit by it. He had evidently met McLuhan at some point on the academic circuit, and corresponded with him now and then; McLuhan had sent him *The Mechanical Bride*, and he lent it to me. I don't think that book was F.P.Wilson country; by the time I could bear to part with it I had left Oxford, and I sent Wilson's copy back wrapped up very, very carefully, as if it had been a Gutenberg Bible. 'Thank you,' he wrote, 'for sending McLuhan's odd book with such conscientious parcelling.'

Perhaps it was Wilson who mentioned to McLuhan that he had an admirer, a rather strange and unsettled young man called Wain who had recently left Oxford to take a lectureship at the University of Reading, twenty-eight miles down the river. Or perhaps someone else did; I mentioned Marshall McLuhan to so many people that sooner or later one of them would be bound to run into him or someone who knew him. At all events, some time in the earlier 'fifties he wrote to me, inviting me to contribute to a magazine called *Explorations* which he and some colleagues were bringing out at the University of Toronto. I wrote a short piece; it appeared; our acquaintanceship was launched, for had I not proudly appeared under his editorship, was I not one of his team of Explorers? In 1956 I sent him my first volume of poetry, *A Word Carved on a Sill* (the first, that is, with a commercial publisher; there had been the conventional limited edition of a 'slim volume' four years earlier), and he replied with a generously appreciative letter.

The first time we met in person was on a wintry night in December 1958, in, of all places, Brooklyn. I was spending some months in America; my curiosity to see more of that country had been aroused by a short and hasty visit the year before, and in the autumn of 1958 I moved my life lock, stock and barrel to America – not on a campus, which would have

wedged me back into an environment I had only recently
summoned the determination to get out of, but simply moving
here and there, keeping alive by writing, finding new places and
new people. I had spent a couple of months in the New England
countryside, but as winter came down I had come into New
York and, with the help of friends, found a small apartment in
Montague Terrace, Brooklyn Heights. I stayed there till May
or June 1959 and have never been back to the place; it was so
pleasant, so quiet, so full of a friendly and unthreatening
neighbourhood spirit that I am afraid to see it again in case it has
been spoilt, sullied, degraded. I remember it with so much
affection, the little shops and businesses and bars, the promenade where one walked and admired the finest of all views of
Manhattan, the view that makes you catch your breath and
think what a wonderful thing it is, after all, to be a human
being. (Actually *being* in Manhattan usually has rather the
opposite effect on me.) Marshall McLuhan and I had been
exchanging letters; he was on a visit to New York and he knew
where I was; the letters became telephone calls, the date and
time were settled and he appeared in person. I can't remember,
at this distance of time, why I received him in the apartment
rather than meeting him in town somewhere, but at any rate he
took the I.R.T. to Borough Hall, came up to street level in the
lift, braved the night and weather along the promenade, and
knocked on my door. With him was a thick-set Irish-American
priest. Marshall made something of a habit of priestly company. As there are some men you rarely see without a woman,
and others you rarely see without a dog, so it seemed to me that
when Marshall appeared there was usually a priest in the offing,
which after all was natural for an Irish Catholic of blameless life
and with no love of solitude.

Of course these priests were always of the jolly, man-to-man
kind, well able to laugh tolerantly at a slightly *risqué* story or
hold their own when the bottle went round. The one he had
with him on this first occasion was very much the type. The two
of them came in smoking cigars the size of cabbage stalks, and

the first impression Marshall made on me was of a kind of all-boys-together jollity. I suppose it was just the dedicated family man and conscientious college teacher enjoying a night out on the town with the boys. He was genial, so determinedly so that he seemed at times to be doing it for a bet, and the cigar stuck in the corner of his mouth made him look like a gangster in a B film. All this I enjoyed. I have never objected to a slight touch of absurdity in people I admire and value; it gives an extra spice to their characters, and sets at a distance the ordinary dullness of life.

The evening passed off agreeably; what we talked about I don't remember, but knowing Marshall I am sure we soon plunged into ideas. When we parted, it was with a promise to meet again soon, and in fact we came together the following spring in Washington, D.C., at something called a Congress of Cultural Leaders, the brainchild of Robin Richman, who was organising a network of events in which various literary and other notabilities criss-crossed the United States. All I recall at this distance of time is a series of isolated vignettes: a reception at the house of Walter Winchell, a party at which Kathleen Raine and George Barker were present – I remember thinking what a puzzle anyone would be setting himself if he tried to get a unified impression of what English poets were like by somehow conflating the three of us.

We were supposed to be discussing the theme of the 'Mass Media'; that would explain Marshall's presence there, because although he was some years away from his flowering of reputation he had begun to be known as a person with interesting views on that kind of topic. I remember his announcing straight off, 'The English language is a mass medium', which had the refreshing effect of broadening the discussion immediately.

There was a lot going on in my personal life at the time, and the subject of our debates and discussions claimed some, but not all, of my attention. The vignettes, however, have stayed. Whose beautiful lawn was I slowly walking across when I came upon the lean, ascetic figure of Father Martin d'Arcy, sitting in a cane chair? Where was the graveyard in which I spent a fascinating hour with Robert Lowell, reading off names and dates and breathing in the ancestral smell of that green and flowering place associated with death, rebirth, renewal, continuity, history? I met and talked with Lowell quite often during the week or so that our deliberations lasted; became aware of the depth of his knowledge of European history and literature, and how much his view of life, and of death, was nourished by the past. I also remember Lowell's firmness. He had a very clear idea of which people he had time for and which he didn't. I once met him when I was in the company of a perfectly pleasant man who worked on the editorial staff of a literary magazine; we were having a drink together, Lowell happened to come in, and when Lowell and I agreed to meet later I suggested that the other man should come along too; I have always been easy-going about such things, no doubt too much so, and certainly to my cost. Lowell trod on the suggestion very firmly. He wasn't rude, but he left neither of us in doubt that the idea didn't appeal to him. The other man quietly bowed out.

That particular scene took place in a certain bar (I have always gravitated towards bars), and indeed I think there must have been one bar I was in the habit of drinking in, because I can see myself very clearly in there with Marshall. He was sitting on one of those circular stools with metal stalks that American bars always have, and he was bringing up a lot of wind. Marshall was a nervous man, not in the sense of being timid (far from it), but in the sense of being highly wrought, possessed by a kind of nervous impatience that made him eat quickly. This same impatience accounted also, no doubt, for the terrifying quality of his driving ('I drive like a bad-tempered cab-driver'), aiming the car at the narrow and irregular gap between two lines of traffic while explaining ('Incidentally, John') some new development in his thinking. It quite clearly explains his tendency to flatulence. Forty-odd years of eating too fast will have their effect; the gods of the gastric juices are not mocked. I can see Marshall now, sitting on the bar stool toying with a glass of beer (and the sudsy stuff they sell you as beer in America would in any case give flatulence to someone who had never had it), stifling a procession of belches, until the man occupying the next stool engaged him in conversation on the subject of how to deal with the problem. Marshall took up the subject with perfect naturalness, taking the man's advice seriously and also advancing rival theories of his own; though he had enormous intellectual pride, in normal relationships he had not an ounce of conceit or affectation in his make-up. Condescension, loftiness, what the English call 'being stuck-up', was entirely absent in him. He would, if occasion served, have started a philosophical discussion with a gangster from a B film.

By the time I returned to England in the early summer of 1959, I had behind me several layers of experience of Marshall: the early years of fascinated reading of his essays, our exchanges of letters, and the man himself in his cigar-smoking hail-fellow-well-met mood, in his quieter, more confidential mood, and finally in his role as a public debater, not yet widely known but already a Cultural Leader. To these layers the next few years added another of more importance, perhaps, than any of them. I got to know him as a family man, at a time when I had begun to be a family man myself.

Not long after getting back to England – on 1 January 1960 – I got married again, and the next time I had contact with Marshall was during the summer of 1962, by which time my wife Eirian had brought forth our first son, William, and was pregnant with Ianto, our second. We were in Canada, and in Ontario, because I had signed on to teach a Summer School on Shakespeare at McMaster University. McMaster is situated beside Lake Ontario in the steel-manufacturing city of Hamilton. I remember that summer as a strange, rather hallucinatory time, not at all unhappy or unrewarding but curiously unreal and dream-like. The stifling heat pressed down, one moved about in a slow, drugged fashion, and the impression of unfamiliar streets, houses and gardens mixed with the thoughts of basic and familiar stories, ideas and characters – for, during many hours of each day, the talk was mainly of Shakespeare – in a thick, sluggish tide that nevertheless pullulated with rich imaginative life.

Hamilton is not very far from Toronto, and Marshall drove out one evening, early in our stay, to bring his wife Corinne to meet us and have dinner. Of Corinne I will only say that of all the women I have ever met she struck me as the one most deserving of the epithet 'gracious'. Courtesy and good breeding shone from everything she said or did. The dinner in our rented house was a success, and the return invitation soon followed. We took the bus into Toronto, carrying the eighteen-month-old William and his impedimenta, and Marshall drove down to the bus station to meet us.

Another vignette of Marshall: standing on the concrete floor of the Toronto bus station, a long, lean figure, his curly hair thinning above a lofty, furrowed brow and attentive eyes, swivelling his head as if trying to look in all directions at once. He had not yet seen us as we walked towards him, and his expression was an interesting blend of watchfulness, irritation (crowds and jostling always irritated him) and a certain detached thoughtfulness as if he were analysing the scene before him as part of some vast, never-ending piece of research on the anthropology of modern urban man.

Marshall and Corinne lived in a pleasant house in a suburban street well shaded by trees, in fact Marshall told me with some pride that the area within which the house stood was officially designated an oak forest. During that hot, oppressive summer we enjoyed their uncomplicated, generous hospitality many a time, and spent hours reclining in the cool of the garden. Classes at McMaster ended by lunch-time on Saturday until Monday morning, and we several times came in, all three of us, to Toronto, where the McLuhan house was thrown open to us as a second home. North American houses are as a rule bigger and more spacious than those of Europe, and though their house was no bigger than would be usual among the Canadian middle classes, it seemed big to us, with its liberal allowance of bedrooms and bathrooms. The McLuhans' numerous offspring had not all taken wing then; Eric, the eldest son, had gone, but some or all of the girls were at home and so was the youngest boy, Michael. I never sorted the girls out, though Eirian had their names and their different personalities tagged within the first weekend. Two of them, who shared a bedroom next door to ours, even managed to be polite and friendly to us when reporting that William had gone into their room and relieved himself on the carpet. To me they were all just embodiments of splendid girlhood, and there was no need to tell them apart, though in late years I got to know one of them, Teresa, on an entirely different basis, that of friendship among grown people.

So the Wains shared the domestic life of the McLuhans, and it has left me with a golden sheaf of memories. Predictably enough, at ordinary family meeting-times such as meals, Marshall never made any attempt to lay aside the contemplative life and appear as the family man. The organisation of the household, the comings and goings and small details of family life, were very much his wife's province. I remember one lunchtime when the girls took exception to a joint of beef that Corinne served up. They said it was off, past its prime, on the way to putrefying. Corinne, the careful, responsible wife and mother bringing up six children on a professor's salary, answered firmly that it was the best quality beef at seventy-nine cents a pound (or whatever it was), and they were to eat it and stop being ridiculous. During this small scene Marshall sat at the head of the table apparently oblivious, meditating on how the specialised logical analysis developed in the sixteenth century by Petrus Ramus had infected the seventeenth-century Harvard scholars with scientific scepticism and thus created a thin, over-intellectualised intellectual tradition in New England . . . or some question equally absorbing. I thought myself that the beef tasted slightly sweet, but I am not a judge of Canadian beef and perhaps if was meant to be like that.

In that garden in the oak forest, another vignette of Marshall: in a short-sleeved shirt, can of beer in hand, sitting in a deck chair and talking. 'Incidentally, John, nationalism is entirely a product of the printing press – it fostered linear thinking and formally drawn linguistic frontiers.' 'You can always predict the next development in a civilisation – the trick is to read the signals – just read 'em off.' Distinguished friends came and went; Northrop Frye seemed to be a frequent visitor, and was it at Marshall's that I met Robertson Davies?

The McLuhans were, in their familial aspect, a somewhat old-fashioned couple, by which I mean that their relationship with their children was along traditional lines. Corinne was very much the patient, attentive, full-time mother; Marshall the head of the family, authoritarian and slightly remote. He undoubtedly loved his children, but he didn't fuss over them. Not that his authoritarianism amounted to much in practice. It rather reminded me of that sentence of S.J. Perelman's: 'He had the air of a man accustomed to giving orders and having them disobeyed.' In some respects he approached the comic-strip stock figure of the harassed father of a household of teenage girls. 'There's no point in trying to telephone our house,' he once said. 'It's much simpler to telegraph.' 'Have you heard about the new after-shave that drives teenage girls mad?' he asked me on another occasion. 'It smells like a telephone.'

Altogether, Marshall was not very much attuned to children. He was a kindly man, but his thoughts and preoccupations were elsewhere. Like all people of this kind, he tended, in the presence of children, either to ignore them altogether or to give them fitful bursts of attention that were slightly overdone. William, only just out of babyhood, was naturally enough outside Marshall's range of cognisance altogether, except in one narrow area. The McLuhans had on the wall of their dining-room an Indian ceremonial mask (at least I think it was Indian; it may have been African or Eskimo). William, on first noticing this, pointed to it and said, 'Man'. This pleased Marshall, perhaps because it fitted in with some anthropological or perceptual theory he was developing (he always did like things to fit in). After that, whenever we all headed for the dining-room, he would bend down to William and say in a tone of mounting excitement, 'We're going to see man, William – *man*!' William's usual response was to smile tolerantly.

These weekends at the McLuhan home have left me, then, with a rich store of memories of the man in his relaxed, unstructured moments. And of his habits. One of these was to sit at the kitchen table and pummel the back of his neck with an electrically driven implement which resembled . . . well, now, what did it resemble? It had the kind of curly cable you see on a barber's electric clippers, but its handle was more like that of a hair-dryer, and the business end consisted of what looked like two small boxing-gloves which thudded rapidly and alternately against anything to which they were applied. Marshall used to apply it to the top of his spinal column, on the grounds that this stimulated the trapezium muscle and also the cerebral cortex. All the time the contraption was belabouring him he went on expounding his ideas as usual, making no concession to the self-administered therapy beyond raising his voice slightly to compensate for the noise, and slip in a few asides like, 'Inciden-tally, John, this blooming trapezium muscle . . . '

Other things emerged in their turn. Once, on a visit to his office at St Michael's College, I noted with interest that one wall was dominated by a huge oar, which turned out to be the one he had pulled in his College boat at Cambridge. To portage such an object across the Atlantic one would need to regard it as of some value; to put it on display in one's study indicates that one is prepared to convey that sense of its value to others. Marshall was in fact something of an Anglophile. His time at Cambridge had evidently left him with good memories of the place. As well as its intellectual discourse he spoke with pleasure of its bodily recreations. Who would have thought that Marshall had been in his day a College hearty, a keen rowing man? But, as we sat in the shade of the oak forest with our cans of beer, he recalled epic adventures on the river, feats of prowess and hardihood; a race against some other College in which conditions had been so severe, in wind and lashing rain, that both boats had sunk. I had a vision of the tall, thin Marshall being the last to go down, his head, giraffe-like, staying above the surface as the boat subsided to the river-bed.

So he talked on, and I was glad enough to lean back and listen. I can't think that he got any stimulus from my company, but at least I was a willing pair of ears. Marshall's reputation in the academic world was, at that time, very much that of a wild man, sometimes amusing and provocative but not to be taken seriously ('McLuhan's odd book'). He did not hold a very important post; the University of Toronto was a staid institution, and the English Department tended to follow a tradition of severe scholarship handed down by such figures as A.S.P. Woodhouse. To some of these people, Marshall appeared little better than a gifted clown. They were of course wrong, and yet there was an atmosphere of outrageous humour, a willingness to push the argument as far as it will go, an abruptness of juxtaposition, that gave his work a (to me) highly refreshing quality of unexpectedness and effervescence. But unexpectedness and effervescence are not qualities prized by severe scholars. They have other goals in view, goals of solid knowledge and carefully buttressed conclusions.

Speaking for myself, I prized the Jack-in-the-box quality of Marshall's mind and personality. Yet, at the same time, it increased my respect for him to find out, during these long summer hours of talk, that his basis in scholarship was thoroughly firm. He had studied philosophy at the University of Manitoba and gone on to take the Tripos at Cambridge. In those days one could not get through these courses in the glib, know-nothing fashion that is common nowadays, when (for instance) the University of Oxford turns out graduates in 'English literature' who have never read Milton. Marshall had then stayed at Cambridge and successfully submitted a Ph D, his title, I believe, being 'The Arrest of Tudor Prose'. I never read this thesis but C.S. Lewis, who had because he had read everything, told me that it was a thesis to prove that all the best prose was written by Catholics and that the art withered at the Reformation. And this, too, would be typical of Marshall, who took his Catholicism seriously and espoused its cause at all times, often leaping out at its adversaries from a totally unexpected position.

Another memory. A former student of Marshall's owned a sailing-boat of some sort, and offered to take a party of us on the lake one afternoon. A mixed bag of McLuhans and Wains assembled on the jetty, got aboard and flapped off before the breeze. Marshall and I were on deck, on either side of the cabin which projected above deck-level. There was a bench on each side, so the logical thing to do was to stretch out at our ease, looking up at the sky, within sound of each other's voices, which as usual meant that Marshall monologued and I very willingly listened. There was a fair swell on the water that day, and I recall lying with nothing in my field of vision except the mast, the heat-hazed sky, and occasional glimpses of the lake as we pitched to one side or the other, with Marshall's voice coming from the other side of the cabin, endlessly developing his ideas.

I think indeed that I had struck him at a moment of immense fecundity, when a mass of apparently random ideas had begun to form into a whole in his mind. He must have been putting the finishing touches to *The Gutenberg Galaxy* and getting ready for the more speculative flights of social criticism that were to take him to the peak of his reputation with *Understanding Media*. Perhaps, by listening so attentively through so many hours – and it was certainly no trouble – I played a small part in helping to ready him for his most spectacular burst of ideation.

I found Marshall intellectually persuasive at this period more than later. Indeed, I look back on the years from 1962 to about 1965 as those in which some traces of influence from his ideas filtered into my own. They are slight, shallow traces and no one would notice them who wasn't specifically looking for them, but I believe they are there in things that I wrote at that time. But I do remember, for instance, being attracted to his notion of a new oral culture which might do more for poetry than the culture of print had done, bringing the poet back into something like the role of the troubadour and slowing down the reading of poetry to the pace of the speaking voice. Not long after I got home, I was asked to speak to the Oxford University Poetry Society and I chose the topic, 'The Poet in the Electronic Age' – spreading some of Marshall's message, as refracted through my tastes and preoccupations, to a new soil.

Another feature of the years immediately following that Ontario summer was that I made a determined effort to get Marshall launched with a London publisher. He gave me, in Canada, a file of photocopies of various essays and reviews, enough to give a publisher an idea of what kind of book he would provide, and with this file I trod the stairs of many a publishing house. But nobody wanted to know.

All in all, I seem to have been regarded, during those years, as the official vendor of McLuhan in England. In 1965 Jonathan Miller, already showing that restless brilliance which has characterised his career, had picked up the message that Marshall had interesting ideas and suggested to me that I should interview him on television in some series he was producing. Marshall was just then on a visit to England, by himself this time, and was staying with us in Oxford. It took me no time at all to decide that I was totally unfit for such an enterprise, and Miller, wisely, got Frank Kermode to do it, thus confronting Marshall with an intellect as well-stocked as his own and with as keen an appetite for speculation. In my capacity as Marshall's bear-leader, I was present at that interview, which was filmed on a sweltering afternoon in a riverside studio in Hammersmith or possibly Richmond. I listened, watching through the glass panel, with interest and admiration but only occasional flashes of comprehension. The discussion operated on a plane so far above vulgar common sense that there were moments when I felt as if I were in a theatre, watching one of those scenes in Thomas Middleton's *The Changeling* which take place in a lunatic asylum. The interview never went out.

Marshall's visit to Oxford, in that year of 1965, provided me with another batch of memories. Some of them will seem trivial, but all are precious to me, as recalling the flavour of the man. I had, by that time, signalled my solidarity with the 'electronic era' by going so far as to acquire a tape-recorder, and we spent some time making a tape of our favourite poems, Marshall reading Hopkins in an extraordinary stop-and-start manner which he claimed was dictated by the poet's own diacritical marks. (I wonder where that tape is now?) Eirian is an excellent cook, and we thought we were feeding Marshall adequately, but it must have been that his accustomed level of protein was not being maintained, for one day he came back from the market with a couple of pounds of steak, which he suggested we should have for breakfast the next morning. We dutifully grilled it, and that is the only time in my life when I have had steak for breakfast, another experience I owe to Marshall.

That Oxford visit of 1965 is also useful to look back on because it helps to date Marshall's spectacular rise to fame. That came with *Understanding Media* in 1966. *The Gutenberg Galaxy* had been much talked about but it was still the book of a literary historian. Marshall had not yet become taken up as a propounder of solutions to social questions. Once he was taken up, he became – for a time – a world celebrity, a sought-after oracle, besieged by publishers and TV networks, and inevitably he tended to disappear from our ordinary life. We were still friends, but my life was never again as close to his as it was during those first seven years.

Already, by the time of my second Canadian visit in 1969, I felt myself beginning to lose interest in Marshall's ideas because they seemed to me to be hardening into a framework, predictable and inflexible. During his first phase, he had been marvellously attentive to the life around him and to what he found in books from the past, marvellously fertile of suggestion and analogy. During his second, which by 1965 had set in, he seemed to me to be doing little else than read books, and observe phenomena, and see where they fitted in.

One of the reasons why Marshall's vogue blazed so furiously and then went out so abruptly was that its fuel was essentially topical. The earlier part of the 'sixties was a time when a great many people had become worried about what the new methods of communication were doing to them. The coming of instantaneous communications, the shift from newspaper to radio and thence to television as the staple means of informing the ordinary person about world events, the consequences for trade of the decentralisation brought about by electronic dissemination of data – all these changes bred uneasiness. And in the world of education it was being noticed, apprehensively, that the youngest generation of adults, the students who were arriving at the Universities, were of a generation that had grown up in front of the television screen, had largely by-passed the book, and were now confronted with a syllabus and a set of learning conventions based on the printed page.

Marshall, like a cricketer taking an unexpected and glorious catch, was in the right place at the right time. Throughout his career as a literary critic he had consistently shown an interest in the affective side of literature, the ways in which it is perceived by, and works on, the mind. He had proceeded with an eye both to the writer and to the reader. In channelling his interests in this direction, the influence of Cambridge had been crucial. If, after graduating from the University of Manitoba, he had gone to Oxford rather than to Cambridge, the whole course of his work would, I am convinced, have been different. In the Oxford English faculty in the years in which Marshall would have been a student, the three most acute intelligences were those of C.S. Lewis, David Cecil and Nevill Coghill. Lewis, the mediaevalist, saw himself as the interpreter of a vanished world, expounding a centrally Christian tradition to the barbarian ears of modernity. David Cecil was the scholar and teacher as *belle-lettriste*, a skilful biographer, a graceful essayist, teaching good style and historical imagination by example rather than theoretical precept. Coghill, with his Irish instinct for the theatre, delved into questions of Shakespeare's stagecraft which were opaque to the conventional academic. Each of them treated the reader, or the audience, essentially as material to be worked on: to be coaxed, to be instructed, to be guided into a position where the richness of great literature was more easily visible to them. Their approach to the reader was, in the best possible sense, didactic. The Cambridge tradition was analytic. The field of literary studies was very much dominated by I.A. Richards; the middle and late 'thirties, when Marshall, already aiming at Cambridge, would have been intensely receptive to what was emanating from there, were the years of Richards' great vogue. And Richards was a psychologist who had turned his attention to literature because he was interested in the cognitive processes involved in reading. Where the Oxford critics worked to set authors in their historical period and to correct errors caused by the distortions of time, Richards was primarily interested in the psychology of the reader, and this concern spilt over into the work of his most brilliant pupil, William Empson, and also to some extent that of F.R. Leavis, who was in the main an opponent; though Leavis complicated matters by regarding literature as primarily character-building. This was the Cambridge that produced such studies of the mind as F.C. Bartlett's classic study *Remembering*, which was published in the Cambridge Psychological Library in 1932; a *milieu* which whole-heartedly took up the study of the perceiving intelligence and the effect on that intelligence of how, as well as what, it perceived. The future author of *Understanding Media* could have found no better training-ground. This early preoccupation with how the receiving mind grasps and constructs bore fruit in his work from the start; in his *aperçu*, for instance, that modern poetry of the symbolist wing was developed in the wake of the newspaper press. A newspaper page, said Marshall, with its scores of unrelated items placed side by side, was a do-it-yourself kit for perceiving the world: you read the discrete items and built up your own picture of the kind of world you were living in. And, with that tendency to give the boat one further push after it was well launched, he added that this kind of poetry was born in France, and that the biggest single influence on nineteenth-century French poetry was the theoretical writing of Edgar Poe, a newspaper man.

Or, again, there was his argument, in *The Gutenberg Galaxy*, that the printing press had ministered to nationalism by making it imperative to regulate spelling, which in turn meant that the differences between languages became much more formalised and clear-cut. French, say, was spoken and written in its fully developed form until one reached a certain frontier, when one switched immediately to Spanish or Italian, also in their fully developed form; whereas, in the old manuscript days when spelling was a go-as-you-please affair, there would be an area of fifty miles on either side of the frontier in which the accepted language was a compromise between the two, with elements of grammar and vocabulary from both.

Willing as he was to explain virtually all the phenomena of a society with reference to how that society moved information, Marshall was ready for television and the electronic media generally. Indeed, there is a sense in which it is quite true that he was ready for them before anyone else was. The result was the perfect blend of the man and the moment.

Understanding Media is, even for Marshall, a fiercely wide-ranging book, dragging the reader breathlessly through ever-widening perspectives in which things 'fall into place' only to fall immediately out again and land in another place. Its effect is, quite simply, intoxicating. To read it is to enter a state very similar to drunkenness in its dislocation of normal spatial relationships and its sudden unexpected juxtapositions. And just as the drunk man believes himself to be continually lighting on brilliant insights, so the reader of *Understanding Media* has the continual illusion of sudden flashes of total comprehension of the world. But, in both cases, the *aperçu* is exploded by a fresh one before it can be fixed by consciousness. Nothing is retained except the sense of having been on a wonderful trip. For about eighteen months in 1965 and 1966, the whole Western world went along on this trip. McLuhan's theme was 'the [approaching] technological simulation of consciousness, when the creative process of knowing will be collectively and corporately extended to the whole of human society, much as we have already extended our senses and our nerves by the various media.' To consider the likely effects of this extension of 'the creative process of knowing', McLuhan says, must involve a discussion of each and every way in which we have used the various media to extend our nerves and senses, since 'any extension, whether of skin, hand, or foot, affects the whole psychic and social complex.' Accordingly, we are given chapters not only on Television, Radio, the Printed Word, the Spoken Word, but also on clothing ('Our Extended Skin'), Money ('The Poor Man's Credit Card'), the Telephone ('Sounding Brass or Tinkling Symbol?'), etc., etc. The whole book has the outrageous all-inclusiveness of the brain-teeming McLuhan I had already admired wonderingly for twenty years, the buccaneering readiness to comment on, and assign a place to, absolutely *anything*; it abounds in throw-off remarks like 'The sewing machine created the long straight line in clothes, as much as the linotype flattened the human vocal style.'

All in all, I would say that the period in which I was closest to Marshall McLuhan was the decade from 1956 to 1966. Our friendship had begun a couple of years before that night when we met for the first time in Brooklyn Heights. It began, as I have related, by correspondence, when I sent him *A Word Carved on a Sill* and he replied with a generously appreciative letter. Perhaps it will clarify what I am trying to say if I put that letter on the page. Here it is in its entirety.

Dear Wain,
    Your book of poems begins to implement and express

your stellar name. And I am exceedingly pleased to have so early a view of the book, to say nothing of your generous words to me on the fly-leaf.

The poems seem to me quite delightful. I like your tough elegance and intensity achieved by such seemingly simple means. You make *terza rima* seem like the most natural means of discourse. Your voice never falters.

I've seen no reviews but shall be very disappointed if there is not a good deal of enthusiasm for your wit and fun. Your electronic brain poem is one I would admire to hear you read. In fact I wish you could get out an L.P. disc of these poems. The sooner professors of literature become disc-jockeys the better!

Would it be possible for you to write a longish poem on The English Revolution of the past 15 years? It seems to me from here that the scope of the changes involved makes the Russian show puny. You could handle the Dryden couplet, I think, very well.

I am about to take off for a few lectures and especially wanted to get this away to you before I left.

Cordial good wishes
Marshall McLuhan

It will be seen that the man who writes that letter is, to his finger-tips, a literary critic. He reads and judges the poems as poems, commenting on their form and texture; he assesses the kind of gift that he takes the writer to have, and suggests an area of subject-matter within which he might profitably work. The interest in oral presentation, the looking forward to the day when 'professors of literature become disc-jockeys', is of course indicative of what is to come. But, at that point, our relationship was along traditional literary lines. I, as a poet, sent my work to him, as a critic, and as a critic he replied.

Six years later, during the summer of our endless lounging conversations, Marshall was still uttering thoughts which I could regard as brain-teeming literary criticism. *The Gutenberg*

Galaxy made its first impact, I am sure, on literary people. This is neatly indicated by the fact that, during the summer of 1962 when it was being prepared for press, the publisher who was to bring it out asked me for what the trade calls a 'quote' to put on the jacket. I have lost my copy of the book (I lose everything), but I do remember that I came up with a sentence that began, 'This is one of the great panoptic books of our time.' I was rather proud of that 'panoptic'. It seemed to me to indicate the quality in Marshall that had originally attracted me, his wide-ranging alertness, his readiness to draw illustration and analogy from the most diverse areas, his 'yoking by violence'. The sentence duly appeared on the book's cover.

A few months after that 1965 visit, the balloon went up. *Understanding Media* was suddenly installed overnight as the essential survival kit for anyone wishing to cope with our civilisation, either to make money in it or just to live with it. For twelve months or more, that craggily speculative book enjoyed sales that went through the top of the bestseller charts. Phrases like 'The medium is the message' and 'The global village' passed from lip to lip, carrying Marshall's name to the furthest shores of the world. It used to give me a feeling of surprised amusement, or perhaps amused surprise, to think that only a couple of years previously Marshall's publisher had thought that a quote from me would help his book to gain attention.

It was to be four years before I saw him again, years in which a great many things happened to him in quick succession (and even some to me). The first in the succession was, as I have indicated, that he became famous and, for that matter, rich. I can date his rise to celebrity fairly exactly from a letter he wrote me on 26 March 1966, in which he speaks of the stampede to interview him and write about him as a new phenomenon which he was still getting used to. I had been told that Tom Wolfe (then a new phenomenon himself) had written an article about Marshall, and I must have had the curiosity to ask him if this were so. His letter says:

You ask of Tom Wolfe. He is a Virginian. A Ph D in
English from Yale. Saw him a good deal in San Francisco
last summer. Shall send you his piece on me. We have been
in *Life* at length – the whole family. Also in *Fortune*,
Newsweek, *Time*, *Vogue* and the rest. Suddenly I'm a
bestseller pet of the College crowds. Must get out some
more while their mood lasts.

That last sentence indicates his attitude during the first wave
of his world celebrity. The cat had suddenly jumped his way,
the cat was an unpredictable animal and might at any moment
jump away again. He proceeded, with gusto, to 'get out some
more'. The next few years saw a torrent of publications, some of
them collaborations with his friend Harley Parker, at that time
Curator of the Royal Ontario Museum. Among the themes the
pair tackled was *Through the Vanishing Point*, a study of the
aesthetic and philosophical implications of perspective. Shades
of *Tennyson and Picturesque Poetry!*

That same letter of March 1966 contains the wry observa-
tion, 'You can imagine some of the local yokel heartburn and
nausea at the calamity of my "fame". Wish you were here to
enjoy the show.'

That sentence dismissing his colleagues as merely envious
peasants undoubtedly links up with a streak of combativeness in
Marshall. Though a kindly and well-intentioned man, he was
not conspicuous for dove-like patience. He did not easily brook
contradiction or scepticism. When, in any intellectual forum,
he put forward his opinion, the implication was 'This is so'; not,
as would characteristically have been the case in Oxford, 'It
seems to me that this is probably so, don't you agree?' Marshall
was not much of a one for asking people whether they agreed.
He stated his view, and if they didn't agree, that was because
they were either being perverse and refusing to see his point
because of some vested interest of their own, or because they
were inadequate.

I don't believe this attitude grew on him in later years. I think it was probably inherent in him. I daresay that as a teacher he was quite autocratic with his students; or perhaps he was as a teacher very much as he was as a parent, adopting an autocratic stance which no one took much notice of. But inevitably his dislike of contradiction, whether or not it increased in his later years, became in those years increasingly evident, as his ideas attracted more and more attention and he had more and more frequently to expose them in debate. I first noticed this tendency in him during that 1965 Oxford visit. In a city where intellectual disputation is such an industry, it was inevitable that Marshall should get into arguments. And when he got into an argument his only way of proceeding was to sweep aside his opponent unceremoniously. Walking along St Giles's Street one day, we ran into Christopher Ricks. I introduced them, and we all turned in to the Eagle and Child for a drink and to sit down. Ricks, whose alert eye had gathered in some of Marshall's doctrines, put forward a few objections and qualifications. He did so good-humouredly; but Marshall's answers were much more brusque. 'I don't think I agree with you about simultaneity being the effect of the two-dimensional and homogeneity being the effect of the three-dimensional.' Or whatever it was. 'That's because you've never considered these matters,' replied Marshall off-handedly. Period. He was not going to say anything else. Another point from Ricks, and another very similar answer. We drank up our beer and left. Ricks did not seem to take offence at all, but I remember thinking that it struck me as a strange kind of tavern conversation between two scholars. But to Marshall, already, opposition was effrontery. And this attitude is not, fundamentally, at variance with the deprecating shrug of 'Suddenly I'm the bestseller pet of the College crowd.' That the crowd should be impressed by his work was not surprising in itself. Nor would it be surprising when they turned their back on him. His valuation of himself was not dependent on popular acclaim. Nor did it depend on the acquiescence of fellow-scholars. Marshall was a law unto himself, and it was that law that he would not have criticised or doubted.

But Marshall's fame went beyond appearing as a calamity to the local yokels. It attracted money, and money changes lives; and lives, in any case, change with time and the twists and turns of personal history. Marshall and Corinne moved to a large, stately house in a select enclave of Toronto called Wych-wood Park. The family grew up and departed. I visited Toronto, with a week or ten days to spare, in the autumn of 1969. Marshall and Corinne showed the same kindness and hospitality, but in other ways changes had set in. The new house was – well, the word that springs to mind is 'baronial'. It had large rooms, high ceilings, and was full of dark wood. Am I dreaming it, or was there a suit of armour in a corner of one of those large rooms, like a solemn, Tennysonian version of 'Man'? Certainly it was a house in which one could easily imagine a suit of armour.

I did not actually stay in this edifice. Marshall and Corinne had a smaller house, close by, which they evidently used as a lodge for hospitality. I shared it with Marshall's younger brother Red. (I have no idea what his baptismal name was; he was always just called Red.) A clergyman, gentle and retiring in character, he had, I conjectured, always been somewhat overshadowed by his older and more conspicuous brother. Certainly I formed the impression that, in their young days, Marshall had rehearsed his role as family autocrat on his junior brother. He himself had set off to England soon after graduating in 1934, and when, not long afterwards, Red was preparing for that European Odyssey which is essential for all young North Americans, Marshall had cautioned him sternly not to let the side down and to remember that he was an ambassador for his country. Above all he had told him, in a phrase that stuck in Red's mind, 'not to turn the place into a hobo jungle.' Marshall's attitude towards hobo jungles was always unbending. He was totally free of any tendency to sentimentalise the vagabond. To him, the drop-out was merely one of the standard products of bourgeois society, as predictable as the commuter with his suburban home and bank loan. 'The Beatnik', he remarked to me in the 1950s, 'is simply the Elizabethan Malcontent.' In other words, those of us who were literate had seen it all before. This remained his attitude to the various phases of hoboism that characterised his later lifetime – from the Beats to the Hippies and thence to the drug culture of the Sixties; all of which, in their turn, produced some reverberations within his family circle.

Much was the same as before – the long conversations in which I mainly listened, the priests of whom there always seemed to be at least one at dinner, and even something of the informality and relaxation. Marshall had bought a tandem, on which he swooped round the leafy avenues of Wychwood Park; and there exists somewhere a photograh of the two of us riding this machine. (Why didn't he get an ordinary bicycle? Was it because he might suddenly have a Thought, as he pedalled along, that he wished to communicate immediately to some faithful Boswell or Sancho Panza sitting behind?) But the old easy-going atmosphere was dead, the swirl of family life, the jokes, the neighbourhood coming and going. Marshall was a great man now, and Wychwood Park was occupied by rich people and guarded by security men. Years before, I had used as the epigraph to an early novel, *The Contenders*, a remark by Anthony Trollope: 'Success is the necessary misfortune of human life, but it is only to the very unfortunate that it comes early.' I suppose I must have seen the truth of that sentence when, at the age of thirty-one, I sent that novel to the press; but now, at forty-four, I was seeing it enacted before my eyes. It was no longer possible to imagine Marshall sitting on a bar stool and discussing remedies for flatulence with just any Joe who happened to occupy the next stool along.

Because I was without the family and not tied in to any particular routine, my time was more disposable on this visit, and Marshall involved me to some extent with his students. But of course the students, too, were different now. They were, I think, all graduates. The University (whether or not as the result of 'heartburn and nausea') had removed him from undergraduate teaching and put him in charge of something called the Centre for Culture and Technology. (A wide-ranging title if ever there was one.) The University of Toronto is a highly traditional body, and I was pleased to note that a flavour of tradition persisted even in the new headquarters wherein Marshall served his strong intellectual punch. It consisted of an early Victorian coach-house, standing in the middle of a yard, dwarfed by the large academic buildings round it. There was something cosy, homelike, makeshift about it. As for what he was trying to *do* there, I take my clue from a letter he wrote me on 11 March 1966:

'Don't miss Ed T. Hill's latest book *The Hidden Dimension* (Doubleday). Big new trend now develops in U.S.A. namely concern with the *effects* of technology. e.g. excitement about the safety-car. It moves on many levels. Most un-American. Most to my advantage.'

Those are, of course, just a few sentences from that letter. It starts with a string of jokes he has heard recently and ends, 'Our love to all of yiz whatever, Marshall.'

Now, it was no longer a question of letters and conversations and the rising torrent of publications. Marshall had a Centre, and a Centre meant seminars and enrolled students and a place in the academic scheme of life. I went to some of the seminars, though I cannot honestly say I got much out of them. Perhaps I would have found them more exciting if I had not had, seven years earlier, those long afternoons of talk, talk, talk, the cans of beer and deck-chairs amid the oak forest. God be with those days. The Marshall I saw now was institutionalised. He had suffered the 'necessary misfortune' of success. Earnest students now came to him as to an oracle, whereas in 1962 he had been the local wild man, apt at any moment to throw off some startling *aperçu*. The earlier role had fitted him better. But as I write that sentence I know that I, too, am less interesting and adaptable than I was in 1962. We all share the same fate, we all cool and harden and become less plastic, and

Custom lies upon us with a weight
Heavy as frost, and deep almost as life!

As for Marshall's method in these seminars, it was basically a formalisation of the old aphoristic deck-chair monologues. He always had proceeded, mainly, by throwing off stimuli; and now each student was presented with a typewritten wodge of thoughts, epigrams, the names and details of books that had influenced Marshall's thinking, all adding up to a do-it-yourself kit for anyone wishing to become a disciple and share the McLuhan insights. The students seemed uncertain what to do with these slabs of typescript. I was uncertain myself. But it was good to see Marshall working, spreading his ideas, receiving even that uncertain homage.

It was not to last. Already he was on a knife-edge. I returned to England at the end of 1969, and a little later came the news of Marshall's brain tumour and the severe operation that was needed to remove it. He told me how many hours he had been stretched out on the table, something horrific – five, was it? Or seven? I remember wondering, no doubt foolishly, whether all that electric pounding on the back of the neck had been good for him; and, no doubt even more foolishly, whether his wildly accelerated mental processes, his restless torrent of analogy and speculation ('the game keeps springing up like crazy,' he wrote once), was not connected somehow with an excessive supply of blood to the brain. I expect these thoughts were as idle and irrelevant as most amateur speculation in the field of neuro-cerebral medicine.

A year or so after his operation, Marshall came to London with Corinne. Their family had dispersed by that time and several of them were on our side of the Atlantic. It was August, the dead middle of the summer, the featureless dog-days when the intoxication of fresh greenness is over and the crisp touch of autumn has not yet arrived. I had escaped from the steamy lethargy of Oxford to the Welsh hills on a family holiday, but to see Marshall and Corinne I took the long train ride south-east, down through the sweltering counties and the baking towns, past the miles of dandelions and ragwort and deep pink willow-herb that lined the stony bedding of the railway lines, and rolled into sweating, stranded London.

We had dinner, with two or three friends, at, of all places, the Reform Club. The meal-time was not an unmixed pleasure. The game of Musical Chairs that had begun in 1965 had taken another turn: then, Jonathan Miller had asked me to interview Marshall on television and I had managed to push the job on to Frank Kermode. In 1967 Kermode invited me to write a short book on McLuhan for the series 'Fontana Modern Masters', which he was editing; again I managed to side-step and the book was written by Jonathan Miller. I thought then and think now that Miller did an excellent job in his brief, lucid study, sympathetic and interested but at the same time trying to get Marshall's ideas into a wider perspective, which inevitably meant questioning some of them and scaling others down. He says himself that he has deliberately adopted 'a hostile tone,' and the book has its contentious side, but by the dog-eat-dog standards of the literary world it is courteous and moderate.

I had given Miller's book a reasonably approving review in *The Observer*, and it was this fact that slightly marred our dinner-party. To Marshall, of course, Miller was simply one of those who had deviated from the plain way of discipleship and assent. Every caveat, every sentence carrying the implication that Marshall could be less than an infallible oracle, was simply a mark of inadequacy, or envious rivalry, or, at best, of 'never having considered these matters.' And the worst of it was that I had reviewed Miller's book, not only without condemning it, not only without sweeping it aside as a tissue of worthless rubbish, but actually with approval. I had recommended people to read it, though of course it was obvious (to Marshall) that such an expedient would lead them deeply into error. I, the 'great panoptic' panegyrist of *The Gutenberg Galaxy*, the original foundation member of the fan club . . . there was a hint of the *Et tu, Brute* in Marshall's accusing eyes as he explained to me, over our lamb cutlets, just where Miller went wrong and how important it was to *realise* that he was wrong.

As the evening went on, Marshall got that burdensome material off his chest and seemed more and more ready to relax and enjoy his holiday and the company he was in. Nevertheless, his so recent and so frightful physical ordeal had left marks on him that were still very visible. He seemed nervous, fragile, tense. There had been some talk of my staying the night with them, and I did in fact accompany them to the flat they were occupying – it was Teresa's, in fact – but when we got there Corinne pointed to the fact that the guest-room was in some sort of inner recess of the house and that to get out – to the plumbing, for instance – I would have had to come through the room in which Marshall and Corinne slept: and the least sound woke him, and he had to be in a totally quiet environment.

I was going back to North Wales the next afternoon, and before I left to find a bed elsewhere Marshall and I agreed to have lunch together in a pub before I took my train. So, about noon, we met again. The pub was a modest place in a quiet side street. It was the era when loud juke-boxes in pubs were just coming in; some had them and some didn't, but it had not yet become *de rigueur* for every pub to greet you with a blast of amplified pop music as soon as you opened the door. That came later. This pub had rather loud music, I think from the radio, and Marshall asked the landlord to turn down the volume. He made the request not ingratiatingly but with something like his old authoritarian manner, merely adding by way of explanation 'We're talking'. The man, for whatever reason, obeyed.

We sat in the suddenly quiet pub and had bread and cheese and beer and talked as of old, one more in that series of conversations, he expounding and explaining, I listening and enjoying the flow and occasionally putting in a question that punted him towards a new pool of ideas: the same series that had been going on for thirteen years since we had first met in Brooklyn Heights. Thirteen years is not very long, and yet I think it must have been a central ridge of my life; looking back, it seems to stretch over an enormous area.

I can't remember what we said, but I recall clearly the feel of it, and that we were as easy as in the early days. Lunchtime over; Corinne came and scooped up Marshall to go home and rest. She was driving a car; hired, I suppose. They got into the car; I stood on the pavement. As the car moved away down the narrow, airless street, Marshall twisted round on the back seat and waved to me through the window with all his old friendliness. I waved back with all mine.

I never saw him again. He lived almost another ten years – till the last day of 1980 – but they were years in which ill-health and lowered vitality largely put a stop to his zapping back and forth across the Atlantic. We corresponded, fitfully, and the goodwill was always there; but after that last London meeting, the relationship between us became one of memory, as it is today. I thought of him often during that last twilight decade, and I think of him often now; with admiration, when I recall the thrust and sweep of his mind, and with affection when I recall his slightly bemused attitude towards that modern world which he claimed, so gallantly, to be able to control by understanding it.

Light Breaks
Where No Sun Shines

THE FIRST MAMMALS, I gather, were nocturnal. When the warmth of the sun receded, and their predators, the huge carnivorous reptiles, became torpid in the chill of the night, the mammals, small and insignificant, emerged from hiding and, clad in their warm pelts and peering about with the large eyes characteristic of the night-dweller, roamed at will through the endless forests of huge ferns and feathery, archaic trees. And when in due course the mammals' restless ambition was crowned and they inherited the earth, they to some extent continued the same pattern. At sunset, many species of mammals rouse themselves, emerge, and during the night hours act out their most intense experiences: mating, hunting, nesting, burrowing, contriving, fighting off their competitors.

Of course not all dwellers in Megalopolis are nocturnal. But, for obvious reasons, those associated with the performing arts tend to be so, since these arts begin to weave their magic when the workaday world has laid down its tools. Actors, musicians, entertainers, inhabit the night; usually too tense to eat before they give their performances, they go out afterwards and find places that serve food late at night, and then places that serve drinks still later, so that they can unwind and conduct post-mortems and generally benefit from each other's company. And where they go, the people associated with them go; their friends and lovers, the critics who write about them, and the agents who want to hire them, and in their wake an entire rag-tag-and-bobtail that just wants to associate itself with their world.

It so happens that I have lived – not just visited, but had a domicile where I was normally to be found, an occupation that I followed, a local habitation and a name – in three of the world's biggest cities, London, Paris and New York. In all those places I have encountered night people. Some of them have become important to me. And three especially are among my companionable shadows.

*

When, in the summer of 1957, I first visited America, I arrived in New York in an exhausted and enfeebled state. The trip had been arranged hurriedly, and my smallpox vaccination, taken only a week before leaving, had knocked me on the floor. (It was the first I had ever had. My parents, in the 1920s, were simple-life, natural-remedy people who disapproved of vaccination). I lay in bed with a high fever until the morning of the flight, when I managed to wobble on to my legs, pick up a suitcase which seemed impossibly heavy, and get myself somehow to the airport and on to the right plane.

Arriving, in this state, in a city as crackling with energy as New York was a strange experience. Riding into the city on the airport bus, I noticed with mild curiosity that the slightly phantasmagoric air that great cities always seem to me to have, the dream-like impression they convey, was intensified by my own fevered perceptions. The skyscrapers seemed to sway in the wind like palm trees.

This being so, it was fortunate that the first new aquaintance I made in America, before I had been there more than a couple of hours, should have been Harvey Breit.

I had been invited to lunch by Victor Weybright, the publisher in charge of the New American Library, a rotund, genial, unflappable man. We met in a little French restaurant called La Petite Marmite, one of those small enclaves of Europe that one finds in New York and accepts as part of the patchwork variety of the place, so that their effect is at once slightly bewildering – one more displacement from straight-line reality – and reassuring, bringing one back to European food, European traditions, European words and ideas.

I entered the place, looked about, located Victor, and saw beside him the man whom Victor had selected, out of all his vast acquaintance, to be my first New Yorker. Physically, Harvey was a man who seemed to be moulded from tough, resilient indiarubber; not tall, but well built; with a round face and head whose roundness was outlined by a greying crew-cut. That was what you saw when you first caught sight of him across a room, but on approaching and actually making contact with him you noticed two things that immediately became the dominant impressions. One was his smile, which was warm, a little lop-sided, and slightly conspiratorial, as if you and he were in shared possession of a special joke – that you were able, perhaps, to see a strand of humour in that situation, that place and those people, which had not yet revealed itself to the company at large. The other was his voice, which was pure gravel.

If you were talking to Harvey Breit and not just standing near him, these impressions were all unified and merged – drawn into a centre, as it were – by the gravitational pull of his personality. He was very close to being that impossible thing, the perfect conversationalist. He had enough in the way of original ideas and piquant anecdotes to keep the talk bowling along if ever it seemed to flag, but he was primarily a listener, interested – or conveying that he was interested, which amounts to the same thing – in the person who confronted him.

He usually had a glass of Scotch whisky in his hand and a fairly numerous company around him, for I never remember his voluntarily drinking anything else or voluntarily being alone. He was volatile, receptive, humorous, appreciative of the quirks of individual personality in a gathering of people, how its energy ebbs here and flows there, how the currents of antagonism and attraction, of agreement and opposition, thread through the mass of bodies like undersea currents in an Atlantic bay. And the inevitable glass of Scotch was part of it too, for there was always about Harvey a hint of the freebooter, the scamp, the truant from the prosaic dailiness of life. His lop-sided grin, his battered voice, carried a suggestion of the Third Avenue bar, the speakeasy, the shirtsleeved companionship of smoky rooms where American males bet on horses, shoot pool, and generally for an hour or two slip the collar of domesticity and the nine-to-five imperatives of their Puritan culture.

Theologians speak of the World, the Flesh and the Devil. Harvey, though doubtless no stranger to the Flesh, did not strongly suggest that its defeats and victories were of central importance to him. Of the Devil, being unusually free of malice and envy, he carried no taint at all. His sphere was the World, and the world he enjoyed and belonged to was the world as it is seen from New York City.

So there we were, face to face in La Petite Marmite, which I found an attractive and reassuring place in spite of the fact that the floor seemed to be buckling slightly under my feet, or was it my knees that were buckling? Food and drink brought their accustomed comfort, conversation did the rest, and I began to feel warm and secure.

During the preceding hour I had had just about time to stop off at my hotel and try to shave, only to find that my electric razor would not fit the American circuits. I had lugged it from England, and it was no more use to me than a broken spanner. I mentioned this fact, perhaps to explain why in addition to being wild-eyed and pallid I was also unshaven, and Harvey immediately suggested that after lunch I should come home with him and he would lend me a spare one of his own. So it happened that the first American domestic interior I saw was the Breits' elegant house in Park Avenue, and that the second new acquaintance I made was Harvey's wife Patricia Rinehart, who was as elegant and welcoming as the house and even more beautiful. She had all the characteristics that set off and complemented Harvey's; her slenderness seemed even more wand-like beside his chunkiness, her gently fluting voice even more musical as against his rich husk, her wide-eyed, cool amusement a counterpoise to his conspiratorial grin. I was to see a good deal of Harvey and Pat, in New York and in London, and every minute I spent with the pair of them was a pleasure.

The background of their personal lives, how they had met or how long they had been together, I never discovered. They had two beautiful offspring who were just emerging from childhood; beyond that, I knew nothing. The money, obviously, was Pat's. In the 'thirties, Harvey had been a needy young literary man like any other – it is a very standard type – and doubtless he inhabited Greenwich Village or at any rate frequented the kind of literary and artistic gatherings that give Greenwich Village its *raison d'être*. The political cataclysms that agitated young writers in that decade, the Depression, the Spanish Civil War, the Nazi–Soviet Pact, all made their mark on the young Harvey Breit; there is an interesting glimpse of him in a book of memoirs by Harry Roskolenko, *When I Was Last On Cherry Street*, which shows him at a weekend conference where writers were exposed to the doctrines of the Communist Party and the radical Left generally. It took place somewhere in New Jersey, a good many miles from New York, and Breit and Roskolenko – such was the simplicity of American life in those far-off days – had no means of getting there except by bicycling. Roskolenko recalled him on the return journey, wheeling his bike because of finally intolerable saddle-soreness, picking over these fundamental questions and still, with all his Socialist sympathies, voicing the misgivings of one unwilling to give up belief in liberal democracy. These misgivings were to surface thirty years later in his only novel. But we shall get to that.

I don't know whether, at that stage, Harvey made much of a reputation as a poet, which was his chosen field of activity, but for the occasional square meal he seems to have relied on journalism. Later, in the 'forties and 'fifties, he was on the staff of the *New York Times*, contributing to it a series of interviews with writers, both home-grown and visiting, that enjoyed some success and were collected under the title *The Writer Observed*. Harvey's easy manner, his knack of getting immediately on to the wave-length of whoever he was talking to, made him the ideal journalist of this kind. But journalism is unremitting, grinding work, dominated by deadlines, and his marriage to the beautiful and well-heeled Patricia must have made it all seem rather superfluous. About the time I got to know him, Harvey left his job at the *New York Times* and became a freelance writer, in prose and verse, while remaining what he had always been, a man about town, an observer of, and participator in, New York life. That city fascinated him. There was no corner of it that he did not know intimately. And of course the Breits Knew Everybody. To go to their house was to meet such a roll-call of the literary and artistic people of the late 'fifties that if I were to write down their names it would sound like empty boasting; and yet, with Harvey there, it never felt like lion-hunting country; he made the impeccable *salon* seem as friendly and lived-in as a neighbourhood bar.

And speaking of bars, part of the fascination that Harvey had for me was that he had been for so long an *habitué* of the night-spots where, among their other attractions, the great jazz musicians were to be heard. Like so many English men of letters of my generation, I had grown up with a particular responsiveness to mainstream jazz. Like many of my generation, I would have been content with Philip Larkin's formulation:

> What calls me is that lifted, rough-tongued bell
> (Art, if you like) whose individual voice
> Insists I too am individual.

Harvey did not have a special interest in jazz, as I did. He merely accepted it, understood it, had an ear for it, in the easy-going unstressed way he seemed to take everything. There was, you might say, no need for him to take a special interest in it, as there would be for an Englishman of my generation to whom jazz was an import, something struggling to establish itself in a new setting: it was, to him, merely part of his background. When, in the 1930s, he spent his nights in the famous Harlem jazz cafés – the Apollo, the Harlem Club, the Savoy, Wells's – he was not doing it solely to hear the music, but because these places with their ever-shifting variety, their raffish openness to all the comings and goings of life, provided an essential setting for one part of his nature.

Harvey used to entertain me with scraps of anecdote and

information about those nights in the jazz world. He had, he said, been in love with the wonderful Mary Lou Williams, who as a brilliant pianist was one of the few women to make a reputation in jazz as an instrumentalist rather than a singer, and how in his efforts to get a share of her attention it had constantly been necessary for him to dodge his chief rival, the large and commanding trumpet player Buck Clayton, at that time a member of Duke Ellington's band.

I drank in all this. It took me back in imagination to the world of the 1930s, to Fats Waller and Sidney Bechet and Jack Teagarden and Chu Berry and . . . Most pleasing of all, it built up for me a picture of the early life of one of my most loved and admired friends, Bill Coleman.

Bill Coleman was a black jazz musician, a trumpeter, who had been born in the rural South and made the expected move to the big cities of the North once he had achieved prominence as a musician. In the mid-1930s he had been a member of a band called Cecil Scott's Bright Boys, and with them had crossed the Atlantic to play a season in Paris. Bill felt so much at home in Paris that he set about making plans to move there permanently, which he achieved by about 1937. That, in very broad outline, is the story of his life. I met him in Paris in the early 1960s; after which Harvey's tales of the Harlem of the 'thirties took on a new interest to me. I knew Bill during the last decade of his life; he was about fifty-eight when we first met; and it was through Harvey that I picked up a sense of what his early years in New York must have been like. He was already successful then. I suppose one of the most sought-after jazz groups of the 'thirties was the quintet known as 'Fats Waller and his Rhythm'. Since it *was* only a quintet, and since the fabulously successful Waller could obviously have taken his pick of many hundreds of capable musicians, it was something of a feather in the young Coleman's cap that Waller should pick him out to play, and to record, with the group on several occasions. When he sailed for France, it was not as a needy adventurer but as an already acknowledged master.

I owe my initial acquaintance with Bill Coleman to three people. One is myself; another, my early friend Edgar Twyford; the third, some anonymous genius in the office of Librairie Plon, the Parisian publishing house.

To take these in order: myself, because when in my youth I discovered, via the gramophone and the grudging ration of radio programmes, the subtleties and delights of jazz (then, remember, very much in its heyday), I had the good taste to single out the work of Bill Coleman as especially rewarding. This, in itself, called for a certain degree of knowledge and discrimination; Coleman was not in the front rank of celebrities. He was a modest, retiring man who had come to the fore simply because his fellow-musicians had recognised his skill and artistry. The finest, and most famous, jazz musicians had wanted him among them. Making the transition to Paris, he had in 1937 made some memorable discs with Dicky Wells and Django Reinhardt.

Eagerly devouring such jazz as came my way, I was already, at the age of sixteen, an admirer of Bill Coleman. And, since his was not one of the names that were ceaselessly bandied about, this is where Edgar Twyford comes into the story. Edgar Twyford played the trumpet. He was, like the rest of us, a Fifth- or Sixth-Former, but he was already a part of the jazz world of Stoke-on-Trent. (Yes, reader, there was such a thing as the jazz world of Stoke-on-Trent. And why not? It was no more remote and provincial than the jazz world of Davenport, Ohio, which nurtured Bix Beiderbeck. Nor more unlikely a cradle for that kind of sensibility than the gipsy encampment in Belgium where Django Reinhardt grew up.) Talking to Edgar Twyford one night, on the damp pavement after some club evening where we had been in search of the authentic music, I suddenly heard him saying that the trumpeter he admired most, and whose style he would most like to copy if he could ever get up to that level, was Bill Coleman. Since this was the first time I had ever met anyone who spontaneously brought up that name, I felt a sense of confirmation. I, as a mere listener, had been enraptured by the Coleman fluency and delicacy, the combination of energy and subtlety that made his improvisations both exciting and reflective; and now, here was a practitioner, someone who knew what it was like actually to play the trumpet, echoing my sentiments.

At the time when Edgar Twyford and I stood on the pavement discussing his genius, Bill Coleman himself was back in America, whither he had been driven by the German Army. (Nothing short of a world war, and the fury of *Wehrmacht* and *Bliztkrieg*, would have dislodged him from his beloved Paris.) By that time, Paris had become his home, his haunt, his inspiration. Many jazz musicians went there, for during the *entre deux guerres* Paris experienced what amounted to a craze for American jazz. The American musicians did not come to London, where they might have given invaluable stimulus to that generation of British jazz musicians who were struggling to get started; the Musicians' Union had decreed otherwise, being afraid that if Earl Hines or Roy Eldridge played a few dates in England, it might put Joe Bloggs out of a job at the local Palais de Danse. Of such stuff were Trade Unions made in those days.

Sometimes, now, I try to imagine the life that Bill Coleman, in his early thirties, lived in pre-war Paris. It was a Franco–American life, of course; many of his professional contacts were with fellow-Americans – fellow-blacks, for the most part – who spent a week or two in Paris and needed his services in getting their music up to the right pitch of energy and inspiration. But, after that week or two, they went back to America, to the security of their regular jobs and their regular surroundings, distasteful as these must always have been to a black man. They enjoyed Paris, breathed its more human air, and went home. Coleman stayed. He worked with French musicians like Reinhardt and Stephane Grappelli. He played in Parisian clubs and recorded in Parisian studios. He had his regular drink in Chez Boudon, the chosen café of the jazz fraternity. He was happy, and he made wonderful music.

In fact I found, when I came to know Bill, that in his own

person he encapsulated and summed up the qualities that had always attracted me to jazz. His energy and expansiveness were the energy and expansiveness of the music itself. He grew up, and learnt his art, during the classic phase of jazz, the 1920s and 1930s. In that phase, it was basically a happy music. A strain of melancholy there was, of course, in its blues vein, and sometimes this melancholy was heart-rending, for like all art jazz arose at least partly out of pain. But when it was not being plangent it was being exuberant, and then the vitality, the inventiveness, the virtuosity were unforgettable. I use that last word advisedly, because although the world at large has forgotten jazz, though it no longer commands a wide public or makes money, though it has been displaced as the good-time music of a younger generation, it is equally true that it is not forgotten. Records of all the classic jazz musicians are always on sale, re-issued over and over. You may have to search around a little to find them, but in every good-sized town there will be at least one record shop catering for the public that has not forgotten jazz.

As the first great generation of jazzmen – Hines, Waller, Armstrong, Beiderbecke, Hawkins, Teagarden – recede into the past, leaving us their music but inevitably becoming, as men, more and more consigned to the pages of history and biography, we are able at last, I think, to see just how extraordinary they were. They came through adversity and neglect; they had to push against a climate of disdain for their music because it had originated among poor and untaught people; where they were black, and they mostly were black, they had to survive the freezing climate of racial prejudice. The older ones among them, such as Louis Armstrong, had almost universally been born and reared in poverty, for jazz was the music of the Southern black man, and what Southern black was prosperous? The slightly younger musicians who formed the second wave may not have started from so far down in the heap, but the Depression struck them just as they came to the height of their powers, closing the clubs and speakeasies where they worked, killing the 'race market' for their records (for the record companies put out a regular stream of recordings, cheaply made and usually badly supervised, intended to sell in the black ghettos and virtually nowhere else, until the white collectors nosed their way in and informed the rest of the world of the riches they had found).

With this chancy and dingy background, the great jazz musicians made their contribution to the world, and, as I say, I think we are beginning to see now, fifty to seventy years later, what a great contribution it was. It would be useless, and indeed tedious, to make comparisons between jazz and the popular music that has supplanted it, but one comparison stands out: the jazz musician had to be a *musician*, able, as a performer on his instrument, to hold his own in any company (I learnt very early in life, at a time when most of my elders and betters dismissed jazz as rubbish, that symphonic musicians never despised their jazz opposite numbers; on the contrary, they were fascinated by the jazzman's ability to improvise, a skill that most of them lacked almost totally). The place of those *virtuosi* has been taken by a race of perfomers who, whatever skills they may have, are rarely musicians. The old jazzmen got up on a platform and played their instruments. If there was a microphone handy they used it, otherwise they did without. That was the limit of their requirements as far as technical equipment went. People listened to them because of the way they played. Contrast this with the list * of equipment needed in the 1970s by a rock group consisting of five performers:

Make	Item
4 Dave Martin	Bass Bins
4 Dave Martin	Double Horn Units
3 Dave Martin	Single Horn Units
4 Dave Martin	Monitor Cabinets
2 Phase Linear	Power Amps
2 Allen & Heath	8 way mixer

* Information from Jim Godbolt, *All This and 10%* (Robert Hale, 1978), a book, incidentally, which contains a delightful photograph of Bill and Lily Coleman.

Make	Item
1 Altec	BiAmplifier
1 W.E.M.	19 way multicore
2 Quad	Power Amps
1 Hammond (B74142)	B.3 organ and stool
2 Leslie	P.R.O. 900 cabinets
1 Moog (D1392E)	Mini Synthesiser
1 Simms-Watt	200 watt Amp
2 Simms-Watt	4 × 12 cabinets
5 Marshall	100 watt Amps
2 Marshall	4 × 12 Lead cabinets
2 Marshall	4 × 12 Bass cabinets
2 Acoustic	370 Amps GA 1009/1279
2 Acoustic	370 Speakers GB 1006/1019
2 Acoustic	271 Amps HA 1056/1062
2 Acoustic	271 Speakers HB 1001/1069
1 Acoustic	Amps GA 1280
2 Acoustic	Speakers GB 1091/1207
2 Fender	Champ Amps A3160/31672
1 Slingerland	Drum kit (chrome): Bass drum 24 × 14, Tom-toms 20 × 18, 15 × 10, 14 × 10 + Hayman snare drums
3 Avedjis Zildian	Cymbals and Stands (22inch, 18inch, 15inch)
10 A.K.G.	D1000 microphones
2 A.K.G.	D12 microphones
8 Electrovoice	Microphones
1 Ludwig	Drum kit (Silver glitter): Bass drum 22 × 14, Tom-toms 12 × 8, 13 × 9, 16 × 16
1 Levin Acoustic	Guitar
1 Acoustic 'Black Widow'	"
1 Gibson Les Paul	"
1 Gibson SG (Cherry)	"
1 Epiphone Custom (Sunburst)	
1 Martin Acoustic (Natural)	"
1 Fender Jazz Bass (Natural)	"
1 Yahama Acoustic Bass Fg300	"

Make	Item
1 Gibson SG (Black)	"
1 Fender Telecaster	"
1 14 × 5 Hatman (gold lacquer)	"
	Snare
1 Pr 15" Avedis Zilidian	Cymbal
1 Premier	Snare drum stand
1 Ludwig Speed King	Hi-hat pedal
1 Slingerland	Tom-tom holder
2 Ludwig	Cymbal stands
4 Slingerland	Spurs
2 Premier	Bass drum pedals
1 Premier	Stool
1 Ludwig	Anchor

4 tuning keys, 2 lengths of rope, 3 toolboxes.

Without all this paraphernalia they could not play a note. Their equipment cost £15,000 (it would be more now) and had to be hauled about by five men, who needed six hours to set it up and another six hours to take it down again.

Bill Coleman played jazz, loved jazz, and, in a word, was jazz. He played to give people a good time, and he himself was one huge walking good time. He radiated geniality. He had a wonderful laugh, rich and all-inclusive. He was tall and strong – in his Kentucky youth he had worked in a foundry, and the powerful frame it developed in him was his to the end – and when he entered a room you looked instinctively towards him.

This is what I did one evening in 1962, at a party in the offices of Librairie Plon. It was, as I said, some anonymous genius in that office who was responsible for my coming face to face, at last, with Bill Coleman. (Edgar Twyford, where were you on that evening?)

I had published, in 1961, a novel, *Strike the Father Dead*, whose central character was a jazz pianist. In searching for a name for this character, I wanted to anchor him firmly in England and in the English middle class (the story to some extent hinges on this), and the name that came to me as most suitable was 'Jeremy Coleman'. Both halves of that name seemed right. At one stage in the story, the action moves to Paris and Jeremy meets a character called Percy, a black trombone player who has made his home there. I did not intend Percy to be a portrait of Bill Coleman, since I had not yet met him, but certainly Bill Coleman was present in my mind as an example, so to speak, of a black American musician who settles in Europe. Percy was my notion of what someone like Bill was probably like, and this must have been another reason why the name 'Coleman' came to mind.

When the book was translated into French as *Et Frappe à Mort le Père*, and published by Librairie Plon, the publishers gave a party to launch it. This was why I was standing in a long room on this Parisian evening, beside a table loaded with food and drink, when Bill Coleman came into the room. I did not know he was on the guest list, which I had not seen, but I recognised him at once, not only from photographs, but because I had several times been to hear him play in the Left Bank jazz club (Les Trois Matelots, I believe) that regularly employed him. Someone in the promotion department of Plon, some unknown genius, had seen in Percy a resemblance to Bill Coleman, or perhaps had merely been told that the book contained a character who was a black jazz musician, and had put Bill's name on the list.

We were introduced, we talked, and the rest was just the story of our friendship, which continued for nearly twenty years. I do not think Bill had read my novel, either in French or English, when he went to the party, and for that matter I very much doubt whether he ever did read it.

That was the beginning of my friendship with this warm, gifted, responsive man who had emerged from a life I could scarcely imagine into a life I could visualise fairly clearly from the outside and, at times, almost participate in. It was a friendship that drew together threads from many areas of my life. There was, to begin with, my fascination with Paris itself. (No, ashen-faced reader, you are not about to be assailed once again with the obligatory hymn to Paris that every English and

American writer warbles out sooner or later.) I first saw Paris as a schoolboy in 1939, and fell in love with the place as deeply as anyone ever did; a few months later, war closed over Europe, and when it was over I was too impecunious to travel, so that it was not until 1948, nine years later, that I got back there again. It was the first foreign city I went to after the years of being island-bound in Britain, and the first I wanted to go to; I had dreamt about it all through the years when I was growing from boyhood to young manhood, taking out my packet of memories – visual impressions of streets, buildings, the Seine, the buses, the plane trees – and polishing them like a collection of enamels. To this day it remains the foreign city where I feel most relaxed and at home, the only one I visit as regularly as the seasons come round, the only one where I have worked with French people and drawn a French salary.

In a volume of linked poems called *Letters to Five Artists* (1969) I included a poem addressed to Bill Coleman, called 'Music on the Water'. The structural spine of the poem is that it describes two long journeys, undertaken by races of men and women under the compulsion of their historical destiny: the black slaves, unloaded from the prison ships on to the coast of North America in the seventeenth and eighteenth centuries, living out their captive lives on the banks of the great rivers of the South, especially the Mississippi, and finally emerging into modern urban life; and the gipsies of Europe, travelling the roads of mud and dust, always at odds with the societies that grudgingly tolerated their slowly-moving wooden wheels, as ready to blame and persecute as the white American was ready first to enslave and later to lynch. In the years just before World War II, a number of classic jazz recordings, mostly by small groups of five or six musicians, featured the black Bill Coleman and the gipsy Django Reinhardt. (Presumably even those who never listen to jazz know that Reinhardt was a guitarist and that he was one of the minority of jazzmen to be acknowledged as a genius by musicians generally.) These two representatives of their unquenchable races met and worked together in the Paris of the four or five years before the Nazis rolled in; both musicians of genius, they caught and held in their music a synthesis that conveys the spirit of the gipsy, the spirit of the black man, and the spirit of that Paris that hung on the bough like a perfectly ripened fruit, driving the *Herrenvolk* mad with appetite.

The poem never made any impression on anybody, perhaps because the subject-matter was too arcane; who, in 1969, knew or cared about a handful of jazz musicians in the Paris of the 'thirties? Or had any ear for what I was trying to say about human history, human art, human interweaving? But, in common with all the poetry I have written, I wrote it because I had to, because the thoughts that inform it welled up in my mind and would not go away until I had sung them aloud, and I am glad to have done so. Paris is a character in that poem, part of which runs:

and Paris in the spring, the cold-eyed spring
hard buds, hard stones
Paris
the cold inexhaustible mother
feeding desire with hard nipples

spring:

time of the dispossessed, the voyagers,
envious only of solitude

Sweet mother who leaves us all stranded
sweet mother who fuels our veins with hate

under whose bridges we crawl
in the rainy night
amorous as sparrows

the dark flowing Seine
inundating our nerve-centres

And Bill this is your second river
channel of paradoxes
ancient passageway of opposites

Le sein is a masculine word:
a woman's breasts, masculine! what a race!
crazy inverted logic everywhere!
le sein is masculine, this is *la seine*,
the drag-net, the bulging tow, the trawl
that disdains nothing, the swag-belly,
full of mussels and contraceptives,
avid of mud, cress and semen,
la Seine, magnet of weightless suicides,
despair of anglers.

The first day, too inert to look for work, I borrowed a
rod and went fishing in the Seine, baiting with blue-
bottles. I hoped to catch enough for a meal, but of course
I did not. The Seine is full of dace, but they grew cunning
during the siege of Paris, and none of them has been
caught since, except in nets.
  – George Orwell, *Down and Out in Paris and London*.

A different river, Bill. But the same need.
Something human to make the cold ripples dance.
Something human out of the bell of your horn.

Aching Paris
those spring evenings in big ugly cafés
staring through plate glass at the clicking street
still unaccountably light at eight o'clock
millions of cigarettes fuming like rockets
the girls with alarm clocks ticking between their legs
timed so as to wake us in mid-orgasm
the pavement sprouting dreams of Martinique

aching Paris, never resting
inexhaustible mother and ticking meretrix
old twisted Paris, gaunt zoo of the poor,
circus ring where the sawdust is milled bone:

Et nous, les os, devenons cendre et pouldre.
De nostre mal personne ne s'en rie;
Mais priez Dieu que tous nous veuille absouldre!

That city has always stirred me up, made me feel more alive, provoked ideas and images to rise from the sediment on the floor of my mind. I associate it particularly with the spring of the year and with the early evening, that hour when the light turns violet and one seems to be breathing pure electricity, the hour when one emerges from whatever side-street hotel one is inhabiting – the Hôtel d'Isly, the Hôtel des Balcons, the Hôtel des Principautés Unies – to take that first *apéritif* and contemplate the stirring into motion of the night-time city. That was the time when I would meet Bill on the nights when we dined together in little restaurants or I went to hear him play in some basement jazz club.

I said that my friendship with him brought together many threads in my life. If Bill was Paris, his wife Lily was Switzerland. She came from Fribourg or somewhere like that, and was very Swiss in her matter-of-factness and her dedicated way of getting on with the job in hand, whatever that job might be. She was also kind and hospitable, qualities I have often found in Swiss people behind their rather impassive exterior. Bill and Lily, so wholly at ease with one another, brought their friends immediately into the circle of that ease. One of Lily's Swiss qualities was the setting of a high value on domestic comfort; Sunday afternoons at their flat in Fontenay-sous-Bois, in the late 'sixties and early 'seventies, talking, drinking, listening to records, and eating Lily's delicious meals, stand out in my mind as perfect islands of domesticity.

Bill needed this background (and he hadn't, by any means, always had it before he met Lily) because by profession he inhabited the night world, which is the opposite of cosy and domestic. He represented not the moody, cafard-ridden, absinthe-drinking side of it, populated by the Nihilist poets staring into their empty coffee cups, but the exuberant, highballing side. He was, as I have said, a walking Good Time. People who knew him lit up with joy when he came in sight. They basked in his genial vitality as in the warmth of a sun, a sun that rose in the dark hours and kept away their chills and fevers.

One evening, towards the end of the 'sixties, I had an example of this that I shall never forget. Bill and I went into a little restaurant where, as it happened, Joseph Reinhardt worked. Joseph Reinhardt was Django Reinhardt's cousin (all gipsies are each other's cousins, but still) and, since Django's death in 1953, was probably the one person whose guitar playing sounded anything like Django's. He was employed at this restaurant to strum gently to aid the digestion of the *clientèle*, and when we went in the restaurant had not long opened its doors and Joseph's guitar was still hanging on the wall. He greeted Bill rapturously – everyone always seemed to greet him rapturously – and the two talked for a while, catching up with the news of their world; then, taking down his guitar, Joseph began to play, unobtrusively at first, but soon, spurred to inventiveness by Bill's presence, with increasing fire and urgency. Bill, who on this evening of leisure was not carrying his trumpet, began to sing the notes that he would have played. The two caught ideas and gusto from each other, and presently the other diners left their tables and, bringing over their chairs, formed a wide semi-circle round them, tapping their feet and enjoying the sound. That was Bill. Wherever he went, people enjoyed themselves, smiled, forgot their troubles, became better friends to one another and to life generally.

I know that is only a small example of the great obvious truth that one of the purposes of art is to bring joy into human lives – that art is one of the things, the very few, the essential, bedrock things that make life worth living and console us for its pains. But it is the example which happens to concern Bill and that part of the night that he illuminated.

One of the reasons, I am sure, why Bill was such a specialist in Good Times was that he had, so to speak, cast in his lot with them. Growing up among the inevitable humiliations of being a black man, a second-class citizen, in the America of those days, he had escaped into the happier landscape of France and put all melancholy associations firmly behind him. It had meant, of course, some uprooting; he had a brother, Ulysses Coleman, who lived in Cincinatti, but I don't believe the two of them met during at any rate the last thirty years of their lives, though they doubtless did so during the period when the Second World War forced Bill back to America. Once that war was over, he was back in Paris as soon as he could get there, never to leave it; except that, in the last few years after his health began to fail, he and Lily retired to an idyllic corner of south-west France, where death finally came to him after a long career of making music and happiness.

Bill's love of Paris must have stemmed not only from the fact that she is lovable in herself, but because the freedom and equality that greeted him must have seemed like coming out of a dingy institution, not quite a prison, perhaps more like the Coloured Waifs' Home where Louis Armstrong learned to play the cornet. Once when we were chatting about food, while consuming one of Lily's great Swiss feasts, he revealed a detailed knowledge of how to cook the very cheapest portions of a carcass, the offals, things like tripe and chitterlings and trotters. When there was a hog-killing, he said, in his Kentucky village, the meat would be cut up on the spot and divided among the citizens, and the parts they did not want would be given to the negroes. I can remember the tone of voice in which he said it, given to the negroes': quietly, casually, with no bitterness and no sense of an effortful holding back of bitterness. In his youth, the black man had been forced by adversity to try to ingratiate himself with the all-powerful white man; in his maturity, he moved into an epoch of militancy and the defiant assertion of 'negritude'; and Bill quietly opted out of both. Of course he was fortunate in the circumstances of his life. Not only are musicians to some extent cocooned from life by their absorption in music; but also, once Bill had taken the courageous step of identifying with France rather than America, his being black gave him, in French jazz circles, a certain *cachet*. In that world, it was the white musicians who had to prove themselves.

Bill's place in his professional world was always assured.

During the years I knew him, he occasionally appeared in large-scale stage shows somewhat on the model of those fronted by great variety artists of the preceding generation such as Louis Armstrong and Cab Calloway. There was one, I remembered, called *Jazz Pour Dieu*, which heavily exploited the black religious tradition in popular music ('spirituals,' etc.). But mostly he worked with small groups or virtually as a soloist, taking along with him his own four-piece group of accompanists. With them, he toured and played dates all over Europe and also worked regularly in Paris. He was an inhabitant of the night-world, as every entertainer has to be; while every night, as darkness comes down, there are thousands in every city who go into that world to play, there are many hundreds who go out to work. Bill's life during the night hours seemed to me a fairly equal mixture of play and work. He fulfilled his engagements, he satisfied the needs of his public; thousands and thousands of times, during his long life, he went up on the stand and gave of his best, showing his appreciation of his audience, giving them something in return for the trouble they had taken and the money they had spent. But there is also no doubt that he was enjoying himself. He had the mark of the true artist in any sphere: one always felt that even if no one had paid him a penny for what he did, it would still have been difficult to keep him away. Jazz, anywhere that brought people together to play jazz and listen to jazz, was his world, and without it he would have wandered off into a limbo.

His usual place of work in Paris was a little dive on the Rive Gauche, close to Notre-Dame, called Les Trois Matelots. Just after Eirian and I got married, at the beginning of 1960, we were in Paris and went to this haunt to hear Bill. It was a year or two before that party chez Plon, and though I had been listening to Bill Coleman for years on record and eagerly discussing him with a whole succession of fellow-admirers starting from Edgar Twyford, I did not know I would ever be anything more than one of his public. We listened and admired; Eirian, who had no experience of jazz and whose musical background was entirely classical, nevertheless had enough musical sensibility to perceive that something exceptional was going on; besides, she was fascinated by the human spectacle, the wordless communication between the musicians, the shared mood that was both relaxed and intent. When Bill was not actually performing, he stood listening to whoever was playing, his tall figure swaying gently, his arms hanging down by his sides, one hand negligently holding his trumpet; and Eirian told me on that first evening that she had particularly noticed, as he tapped one foot to the prevailing rhythm, how dainty his feet seemed: small, for such a big man, and elegantly shaped.

She had plenty of other opportunities to observe Bill's dainty feet, because we went to hear him many times – at the Trois Matelots, and later in London at the Six Bells in Chelsea and at a pub in Seven Dials. But the Trois Matelots is the one that stays most firmly in memory, because it was so intensely Parisian, and Paris was Bill's world. To go to hear him there was to enjoy an evening of contrast. Up at street level, everything that one saw was Paris, and classic Paris at that – the flow of the Seine glittering with lights, the dramatically floodlit Notre-Dame, and near at hand the Boulevard St Michel, the Pont Neuf, the big cafés, the shops I frequented like Gibert and Shakespeare & Co. Once down the steps and all impression of nationality vanished – you were in any jazz spot in the world, with the bar, the tables, the casual customers, the musicians grouped on a small platform no more than eight inches above floor-level.

Bill's music, too, was an affair of contrast. It was full of energy, restless and inventive, and his big chest and strong build enabled him to play high notes with what seemed no effort, so that his note was often soaring. Where Louis Armstrong, that great showman, tended to dramatise his high notes, building up to them, almost saying to the audience, 'Watch out! – Here's a high note coming!' Bill just went straight up, as if playing top C on a trumpet was no more than playing it on a piccolo. But of course he never did it for effect, only in the service of his fertile imagination.

The critic Charles Fox once wrote that the essence of a solo by Coleman was its mobility. His improvisations never come to rest. As soon as one idea has achieved recognisable structure, he is off on another, not with any stumbling effect of having too much to say and interrupting himself, but with a pantherine assurance.

Yet behind the assurance there is always something gentle and self-effacing, something off-hand in his phrasing, as if he were saying, 'Don't attend to me, attend to the music.' He never tried to 'lead' the band, with flamboyant gestures, as trumpeters often do; he simply carried them along with him. He was a musician's musician.

All this time we have left Harvey Breit waiting in the wings while we circled off in search of jazz and Paris and Bill Coleman. But Harvey won't mind: he will have a glass in his hand and be talking to people around him, talking and listening. He always did contrive to suggest that he had plenty of time and could afford to let things move at their own pace. At about the time I got to know him, he had entered on the life of a man of leisure, but I expect he always gave that impression even when he was a working journalist with places to get to and deadlines to meet. The expression 'laid back' had not yet come into being when I first met him in 1957; it was a product of the hippy era which was still just round the corner. But if the word did not exist, the thing did, and Harvey was the supreme embodiment of it.

It was, in fact, *The Observer* that had sent me to America on that 1957 visit; and this will mean another excursion before we come back again to Harvey. I was, at that time, writing regular criticism for their literary pages, and they had decided to run a series of articles on what was in those days called 'Commitment'. This was a fashionable term in the 'fifties, when it was usual to believe, or at any rate to say, that no writer could be worth anything who did not have a political creed and push that creed in his or her work. To be approved of you had to be 'committed' – which meant, of course, committed to the Left. A writer who had thrown in his lot with the Right was out of court in any case; not a very sensible attitude, though the rudeness and arrogance habitually shown by such Right-wing figures as Evelyn Waugh did nothing to correct the imbalance.

In the summer of 1957, then, it was decided in the *Observer* office that this series should be concocted by myself and Philip Toynbee. I was to conduct the interviews with American writers, he with French ones, and he would also do the final editorial work on the series; when my pieces appeared they were apt to contain sentences by him, which is one reason why I have never reprinted them. My brief was to interview Arthur Miller, Edmund Wilson, Ezra Pound and Ernest Hemingway. I saw them all except Hemingway, who wrote courteously from his Havana address to say that he could not break off his work to give interviews, but made a few helpful suggestions as to people I ought to meet. One of them was Harvey Breit.

I did succeed in meeting, and talking at length with, Arthur Miller and Edmund Wilson, and my articles on their opinions duly appeared in *The Observer*. Both meetings are pleasant to recall, that with Wilson because it inaugurated a relationship I valued, and that with Miller because it involved a delightful lunch in the garden with him and his wife Marilyn Monroe. With Ezra Pound, the case was somewhat different. I saw him, but I didn't, except at meeting and parting, actually talk to him.

As most people are aware, Pound's sympathies with Italian Fascism had led him to use the facilities provided by the Italian state radio to put across his views on economics and politics, and when American entered the war in 1941 he continued to broadcast, which made him technically a traitor. After his capture by a unit of the American army in 1945 it was expected that he would be put on trial for his life, but after his repatriation a panel of doctors found him too mentally disturbed to be able to plead, and he became a patient at St Elizabeth's Hospital in Washington DC. I accordingly sought him there; I probably would not have got to him but for the prestige of *The Observer*, for during all the years of his confinement his wife, Dorothy Shakespeare Pound, kept watch over him and filtered all applications to visit him. The name of the paper got me as far as seeing her, and I must have convinced her that I wasn't going to offend or upset him, because I was rubber-stamped through and found myself, on a sultry afternoon, wandering through the enormous grounds of the hospital in search of the poet, having been told no more than that he spent the afternoons in the open air and would be somewhere in the grounds.

Mental patients, as anyone knows who has had any contact with them, most of the time look and act exactly like everyone else. The grounds were full of people strolling or sitting, the tennis courts were in use, and as usual it was completely impossible to tell which were the patients and which the visitors. I walked about for a quarter of an hour without seeing anyone who looked in the least disturbed or abnormal in any way. But then, rounding a corner of the shrubbery, I almost stumbled into a group of figures, sitting in a rough circle, who struck me immediately as the type who would need attention in a mental hospital. They were sitting very still, with downcast eyes and listless expressions, and as I drew near one girl stood up and glided away, with her head hanging down as if she were in the last stages of depression. I was about to pass by, compassionately, when I noticed that the circle had formed itself around a strongly-built man with a grey beard, who sat in a deck chair while the others sat on the grass. This man, stripped to the waist, tanned, of authoritative bearing, was talking in a slow, deliberate voice and the others were listening.

Obviously I had found the poet. The other people there were his devoted circle of adherents, most of whom visited him every day and none of whom were patients at the hospital. The girl who had glided away at my approach, and whom I would have diagnosed with absolute certainty as manic depressive at the lowest point of the depressive phase, was in fact the group's informal hostess, who produced coffee and biscuits for each new visitor. I took my place among the others and gave heed, partly to Pound's voice, partly to my own impressions.

The master plan of this series of *Observer* articles, as I have said, was to establish which of the leading writers of the day were, or were not, committed. Since the word 'committed', in American English, has exactly the same meaning as the word 'certified' in British English, I already knew enough not to march up to Ezra Pound and ask him if he was committed.* I had indeed no very clear idea, in advance, of what I wanted to ask any of my authors; my plan was simply to let them talk and explain themselves, which literary people are always ready to do, and it worked well enough. In the case of Pound, however, there was also the question of his mental state. It was, at that time, an article of faith in the literary world – not merely among the Poundian *cénacle*, but very generally – that Pound was as sane as anyone else and that he was merely being held in an asylum to avoid the necessity of punishing him for treason. Whether anything written by me in *The Observer* would have been able to make a dent in this belief, which was not drawn from any evidence but merely an assumption based on deeply rooted attitudes, I shall never know, because nothing in the end did appear. Pound, like Hemingway though for different reasons, was not among my trophies when I returned. I spent a couple of hours in his company, but nothing resembling an interview took place.

The poet sat in his deck chair, the sun shining on his burly torso. At the age of (by my reckoning) seventy-two, he was magnificently preserved. His muscles had nothing of the stringiness usually found in an old man's, and, though from first to last I did not see him standing up, I knew without needing to be told that his posture would have been straight.

---

* Donald Hall in *Remembering Poets* (Harper & Row, 1979) has me actually asking Pound this fatal question, a pardonable lapse of memory when writing up a conversation we had had in a London pub twenty years earlier. Hall's excellent book gives the best account I know of what Pound must have been like in his last days, after his release in 1958.

His voice, too, was entirely firm, a slow, emphatic, rather old-fashioned American voice. He was uttering a monologue, a steady succession of sentences which went on throughout the whole two hours, without hurry but equally without intermission. The subject of the monologue was his experiences in England in the years just before 1914. Names like 'Fordie' and 'Lewis' cropped up frequently. I had, and still have, no means of knowing whether this was the subject he usually monologued about, or whether he had half-a-dozen habitual themes and this happened to be the one he chose today, or whether – a third possibility – he had been told that there would be an Englishman present and this had jogged his mind towards an English theme. After all, England had been the scene of his heyday both as man and as poet. Whatever faults he discerned in English society, at the time and retrospectively, he had done his finest work there: the Imagist poems, the 1912 translation of *The Seafarer*, *Cathay*, *Personae* and, above all, *Hugh Selwyn Mauberley*. After he left England, first for Paris and then, of all places, Mussolini's Italy, the proportion of the first-rate in his work became thinner and more chancy. So, through that humid afternoon, with the sun glowing down through the hazy air that rises from the Potomac, I sat in silent fascination as Pound recalled the days of his inspiration, the days when the stream of his genius ran fresh and clear, when Yeats took his advice and Eliot accepted him as *il miglior fabbro*, when the world was new and nothing seemed impossible.

It was a very moving experience. But it was not an interview. I felt I could have summed up what I had to tell *The Observer* in three words: *Pound is committed*. To hold a conversation, in the normal sense, with him was out of the question. Most of the circle were silent throughout, but one or two tried to get in with queries, and the only way to do it was to interrupt him with a determination that went quite beyond the normal bounds of politeness, the verbal equivalent of throwing a spanner into a piece of machinery. When this happened – and even the most resolute questioner didn't do it very often – Pound would stop speaking, stare blankly ahead of him, pass his hand over his eyes as people do when they are conscious of great strain, and then begin speaking again. The resumed discourse would never have the slightest connection with the question, nor with what he had been saying before the question. The effect was exactly like that of lifting a gramophone stylus off a record and putting it down arbitrarily at some other point.

I heard, at about that time, that Pound had said to a visitor, 'The top layer of my mind is gone', and this seems to me a good rough-and-ready way of describing his state. Certainly I would not, if the decision had been mine, have turned him out to fend for himself. (Nor was he, of course, ever so turned out. After his discharge from St Elizabeth's in the following year, he was for the rest of his life looked after as carefully, though doubtless in more agreeable circumstances, as he ever had been in the hospital.)

The journeys were made, the interviews, fruitful and otherwise, took place, and my overcrowded ten-day visit was at an end. I had not by any means recovered my health after that initial fever – as fast as my strength came back, I dissipated it in that breakneck programme of activity – and the last morning of my stay found me winding my uncertain way along Park Avenue to return Harvey's razor.

The Breits employed a stately black woman as their housekeeper or chatelaine or whatever the appropriate word would be. This sable Amazon opened the door and surveyed me with a good deal of suspicion. Standing there with Harvey's shaver in my hand, I explained that I had come to see Mr Breit. She left me standing on the pavement while she went up and reported. Her actual words, as Harvey afterwards told me, were, 'There's a man asking for you, Mr Breit. I think he wants to sell you a razor.' The worthy woman obviously took me for a piteous human wreck from the nearest hobo jungle, who had managed to steal a shaver and was trying to sell it to raise money for the next drink. As it turned out, I had the next drink with Harvey and Pat in their beautiful living-room.

Could I have foreseen it, the time was not far distant – about seven years – when Harvey himself was to have his last drink in that room. Some time about 1964, he and Pat broke up, and the next time I saw much of him, in the early summer of 1965, he was living alone in a much less grand, though still perfectly comfortable, habitation. It consisted of what I think property agents call a 'studio flat', one large room with subdivisions made by folding doors, and Harvey's personality seemed to have shrunk slightly in adaptation to his more modest circumstances. He was, of course, older, for it was a good five years since I had seen him; his matchstick-length hair was now unmistakably grey, and his resilient, rubbery body seemed to have grown slightly smaller and spread out sideways. That was what you noticed on a first impression; and though within half an hour the old genial openness had once more taken over as the dominant flavour of the man, there was still an undertone of discouragement, of that shadowy lassitude that descends on people who feel that somehow their lives have gone irreparably wrong.

He was keeping the flag flying, maintaining a man-about-town exterior; on his dressing-table was a photograph, signed with an affectionate inscription, of a deliciously shaped girl in a bikini. But these were gestures. Harvey – now, I should think, in his late fifties – was running out of energy. He seemed to have returned to something like the pattern of his old free-wheeling, night-cruising city life, but on a reduced scale. Under (presumably) economic pressure, he was writing for the papers again, and as far as I could gather baseball was one of his topics. Certainly he spent long afternoons hunched in front of the television set, watching the World Series, and afterwards he would be for hours at the typewriter, analysing and reminiscing. There had always, I realised, been a suggestion of the sports writer about him; he was knowledgeable about the turf and the prize-ring as well as baseball, and I now saw his life, suddenly, as an American version of the life portrayed by the French Impressionists, who were so drawn to scenes of leisure and casual gregariousness, who loved to paint people sitting at café tables or jockeys walking their horses round the paddock.

I stayed with him in that studio flat for a couple of springtime weeks. We talked as of old, and I enjoyed his company as of old; he was no longer the centre of a flashing kaleidoscope of the clever, the beautiful, the worldly; he was just Harvey now, the man himself, with that casual friendliness, that slightly weathered air of having been everywhere and done everything, so long as the everywhere and the everything were within the world of the big city; and all rounded off by that grin that seemed to convey that in spite of having seen so much of the human race he still liked it.

He stayed in the flat a good deal, watching television or reading – he was, I recall, spending a lot of time with a paperback anthology of seventeenth-century English poetry – and, ironically, it was I who went out more into the night-time city, often coming back and letting myself in after Harvey was asleep. It was, I think, the last season of my youth – I had had my fortieth birthday a few weeks before getting to New York – and the youthful appetite for adventure was still on me, blazing, perhaps, for a last time before it went out.

Nowadays, as my energies ebb gently away, I live by the natural sun. These are memories of those episodes of my life that were lit by the neon sun of the city, that glows into garish light as the earth turns its dark side to the day. But this light-within-darkness is not merely a matter of switches and bulbs, power-stations and cables. There is a sense in which all life, and particularly the life of the mind, is dependent upon this self-created light, the light burning within a space which Nature has decreed shall be dark. When I was nineteen or twenty I was passionately fond of the poetry of Dylan Thomas, particularly the early work collected in *18 Poems*. In the classic fashion of the adolescent, I used to walk about on rainy nights murmuring his lines to myself. One poem in particular hypnotised me, the one that begins

Light breaks where no sun shines;
Where no sea runs, the waters of the heart
Push in their tides;
And, broken ghosts with glow-worms in their heads,
The things of light
File through the flesh where no flesh decks the bones.

had only the vaguest notion of what these lines 'meant', but
all those early poems are about the life of the body and the
instincts, the strong, surging, brooding interior life that is
independent of the outgoing mind; they link human fertility
and creativity with the blind thrust of plants and the succession
of the seasons, they speak of 'the force that through the green
fuse drives the flower' and 'the rainy hammer/Swung by my
father from his dome.' They are the utterances of a youthful
poet aware of enormous forces within his own being, forces that
link him to the forces that drive all life onward, and conscious of
nothing very much in the way of ideas, only of the impulse to
song.

In 1965 I published a book-length poem, *Wildtrack*, which
ranged over everything of importance I wanted to say, and
though it has gathered a little dust here and there I find, when I
go back to it, that my essential beliefs and attitudes are still what
they were then, and that the poem speaks them clearly enough.
In it I have two emblematic figures, the Day-Self and the
Night-Self; the one typifies the outward-looking mind that sets
up political and social structures, the other the mind that
dreams, responds to instinctual tides, and harbours myth and
symbol. The poems of Dylan Thomas that spoke to me so
strongly at the end of my boyhood are poems of the Night-Self.

The Manhattan night through which I roamed in that season
of restlessness was one of the places in which 'light breaks where
no sun shines.' And the most memorable thing that happened to
me was an encounter, during the long sleepless hours of one
night, with a poet who knew and explored his own darkness.

*

I had met Robert Lowell, as I mentioned in the essay on Marshall McLuhan, at that strange 'Congress of Cultural Leaders' in Washington in the spring of 1959. And I was to see a good deal more of him in the years between about 1967 and his death; usually in Oxford, often at our house, where he many times dined and sometimes stayed a day or two. But this one night in 1965 marked the breakthrough in our relationship. It lasted most of one night, and in it we talked endlessly, and totally without reserve. We were not alone. We had something better than being alone, for the one other person present was a woman, who was giving off sympathetic vibrations.

Robert Lowell (I never called him by his familiar name, 'Cal'; it seemed to me too silly a name to apply to a man I respected) was a complex man with a complex mind – a mind, indeed, over whose complexities he had, for some of the time, too little control for the ordinary purposes of life. I was always content to take the side of him that he happened, at the time, to be presenting to me. Occasionally he could be in a hard, competitive mood, when his manner would be curt and aggressive, and during these spells I never attempted to fight back, just said very little and hoped for better luck next time I met him. I usually got better luck next time. When nothing happened to arouse the sleeping bandit in him, his prevailing facet was a gentle responsiveness, a warmth, a wish to give. What he gave – to me, at any rate – was always a share of the wealth he carried in his mind: his immense reading, his imagination, his sensibility.

Although that night will live with me forever, there is not, in terms of objective fact, very much to tell about it. We had been invited to a dinner party by a hospitable young woman whose means enabled her to afford a magnificent apartment. The guests numbered eight or ten; I can only remember Lowell and his brilliant wife Elizabeth Hardwick; the others, I recall, were all interesting people who had made names for themselves in one way and another, and yet the intervening twenty years have blown them away from my mind like smoke. I remember Mrs

Lowell talking to me, penetratingly but with good-humoured tolerance, about a review I had recently published, in the *New Republic*, of Lowell's most recent volume, *For the Union Dead*. (I had praised it, but just this side idolatry.)

The meal ended. The talk went on. Various coffees and brandies were consumed; it went on still. Guests began to take their leave. One of those to leave was Mrs Lowell, evidently preferring to get to bed at a sensible hour rather than wait till it suited the poet to leave the flow of talk. In the end, only three of us were left: Lowell, myself, and our hostess. We talked. We ranged over poetry, ideas, reminiscence, back to poetry. Lowell's face wore that expression which has stayed with me as most characteristic of him, a look that blended suffering and happiness in a way I have never seen on any other face. When he was thinking, pinning down an idea or reaching out for the right words, he looked down or towards a corner of the room, and his eyes at such moments were full of an intensity that might, at other times, have suggested pain; then, when he had found what he wanted, he would turn his eyes straight on to your face, and they would be lit with joy.

We talked on. After about the second hour our hostess settled herself companionably across Lowell's knee. It was the era of the mini-skirt, and I remember how, as he talked about Philip Larkin's poem 'Mr Bleaney' and recited passages from it, he beat time on her marble-smooth thigh. We talked for a long time about Philip Larkin, and a long time about the poet Larkin loves most of all, Thomas Hardy. At one point Lowell broke off in the middle of a statement, looked straight at me, and said, 'I don't suppose either of us will ever forget this night.' Certainly I have not forgotten it in twenty years, and if I live another twenty I shall still not forget it.

Though the *timbre* of our talk survives in my head, I don't, after twenty years, remember all the substance of it; still, certain things have not washed away. We spoke of Ezra Pound, and Lowell, who was not in the habit of lavishing much praise on critics, expressed warm appreciation of George Fraser's short book on Pound in the 'Writers and Critics' series published by the Scottish firm of Oliver and Boyd. It is indeed an excellent brief study, and I was glad enough to acquiesce in praising it, though I had recently received a mauling at Fraser's hands; he seems to have decided, at a period when he commanded a very wide audience as a critic, that my work had been over-praised and set himself in no uncertain terms to redress the balance. But we agreed in praising the Pound book, and Lowell went on to say, patting our hostess's delicious thigh by way of emphasis, that it seemed to him worthy to stand beside Henry James's classic short study of Hawthorne. I had not at that time read James's little masterpiece, three parts critical essay to one part biography, so I encouraged him to describe it to me, which he did, and said that it was one of the books that made him proud to be an American writer. When I did get round to reading it, I could see how strong its appeal to Lowell must have been, since, apart from being a rare distillation of the art of the critic, it is also the finest account I know of the New England tradition and temperament. Hawthorne's fiction is built from the essential materials of that tradition and temperament; James's account of Hawthorne's fiction extrapolates and describes, so skilfully that nothing is lost in the re-statement. It is the perfect example of a critic allowing the author to speak first, and then summing up the spirit of what has been said. Whenever I dip back into that little book, as I do often, I wish I could go back to that night in 1965 and engage in a real conversation about it with the New England poet of my own time.

During the last hour or two of our conversation, till about three or four in the morning, I had been steadily drinking bottled beer, as the only drink there was left in the apartment. By the time it was decided that we should all get some rest, I was too sleepy to trek back to Harvey's, and our hostess gave me a superbly comfortable bedroom. As I was sinking to sleep she came in with the friendly information that she and Lowell had decided to crown the occasion by going to bed together in her room, and the still more friendly invitation to join them. I had no difficulty in declining the honour. Even in youth, when one makes a virtue of variegated experience for its own sake, I had never been drawn to these exploits *à trois*.

And so it was back to Harvey's, and baseball on the television, and Seventeenth Century English Poetry lying about in the bathroom, and the ceaseless casual interchange about life and books and people. One day I was in the flat when Harvey and Pat's two children swooped in to pay him a visit. I remember them as about twelve or thirteen, that kind of age: beautiful, lively budding human beings who filled the flat with energy and laughter before swooping out again. Obviously growing up with a sense that the world was at their feet and nothing was out of reach, they seemed like messengers from a kingdom of good fortune that Harvey would only see, now, from the outside. His attitude to them seemed to be one of affectionate amusement.

Almost every situation, however dour, has its positive side, and Harvey's new life of more solitude and more financial stringency seemed likely to benefit him as a writer. He was already back in harness as a journalist, and he had brought out in 1964 a novel, *A Narrow Action*. Its story, set in Cuba, seemed to be a shadowy diagram of the life of Fidel Castro, newly arrived in Havana and at that time still legitimately a hero of the Left. This novel showed me another facet of Harvey. It revealed a man who had reflected deeply on contemporary world politics. He wrote it at a time when Castro had newly come to power after his years of heroic struggle against the vile Baptista, come to it on the crest of the natural longing of the people for freedom and justice, an end to terror and slavery. But from the start, at their deliberations, the inevitable Soviet representative is there, dish-faced, immobile, representing the power that can make or break any régime calling itself Marxist. Castro's sad and foredoomed slide into being a Soviet catspaw is prefigured, in this forgotten novel, before it happened. I recommend the book to students of Latin America.

What it was about Cuba in particular that engaged Harvey's

interest I do not know. After all, there were great areas of his life that I knew nothing about; perhaps he had spent some time there; perhaps that was how he came to know Hemingway, who lived for years in Havana until this same Castro made the place too hot for Yanquis.

Certainly Harvey the novelist had learnt his primary lessons from Hemingway; that is evident, I think, even in such a brief extract as the following. (Felipe is the Castro-figure, Manuel his brother; the time, a few days after the revolutionary government has come to power on a wave of idealism that is already giving way to *Realpolitik*.)

He walked past the guards and into the conference room. A once-plush semicircular bar, mirrored and resplendent with bottles of Scotch, bourbon, rye, gin, vodka, vermouth, brandy, and various kinds of rum, duplicating themselves in the glass, welcomed him and it seemed to him the right thing. He poured a water tumbler full of the dark Jamaica rum, took half of it in a prolonged swallow, approved the dimness of the room and sat down near Manuel. They stared at each other, Manuel with his hands on his lap, Felipe with an elbow on the table and his head against his hand, holding the rum close to his hair. They watched each other like poker players. Then Felipe, said, his eyes half-closed, 'You are too gloomy.'

'I am,' Manuel said. 'Did you hear about Navaja?' Manuel shook his head. 'You could not have, because it occurred at five this very morning.' Felipe said nothing. 'The patrol boats caught him. He was on a thirty-foot yawl with his whole family, a gallon jug of water, some beans, and chocolate. He would not stop when the patrol boat hailed him. They had to shoot.'

Felipe hit the table hard. 'Why did he have to run?'

'They killed one of his babies.'

'What did he expect?' Felipe hit the table again. 'A pat on the head, a gold star? Why can't they have faith?' Furiously he turned the radio on to the Voice of the Revolution channel. ' . . .receiving massive aid from the mighty Soviet Union' – it was Simon Rand's voice – 'we will show the world that a small peace-loving nation can survive and lead the way for all peace-loving peoples without the aid of the Yankee imperialists. Comrades, we have a great leader and in a difficult time we must not be riddled with doubts.'

What doubts, Felipe thought, the same as Fuensanta's? He felt the pain of acidity very high in his chest, almost at his shoulder: the new area of blight.

But at one point Harvey's novel goes outside Hemingway's terrain. It includes a poem, supposedly written by one of the characters, that I found, and still find, touching and memorable. I quote the whole:

A FINAL VILLANELLE

Once I was young and drank all the wine!
I slept on a bed in a budding grove.
Two loves I had, now neither is mine.

When I sowed discord I paid my just fine,
Then went to sleep with the sleeping dove.
Once I was young and drank all the wine!

Now I am older I know nothing's my own,
Except cold bones that sleep by a stove.
Two loves I had, now neither is mine.

Behold: The world's pearl turns into swine
And I find no sleep in the fancies I wove.
Once I was young and drank all the wine!

Landscapes are bleak, stars yield no sign,
Though once I slept in a bed of mauve!
Two loves I had, now neither is mine.

Terez, you were the color, Freedom the line!
This was the oeuvre I had chosen to love.
Once I was young and drank all the wine!
Two loves I had, now neither is mine.

Does that poem touch me simply by its own power, or because it seems to me to reflect, movingly, the state of Harvey's mind and life when he wrote it? I can't tell; it is too late for me to go back and not know anything about Harvey, to treat him simply as a name on the cover of a book; and in any case I have come to believe that to string a barbed-wire fence between an artist's biography and his work is to involve oneself in endless futility and niggling.

Another week or two went by, and then it was time for England, and Oxford, and Harvey once more joined that category of friends with whom I kept in touch by air-letter.

In 1965 I must have written to tell him that my wife Eirian was to have a baby – it was to be our third son, Toby – next May, and his answer gives a characteristically generous response and also ventilates some of his private dissatisfactions. After spending so much of his life in New York, after taking so many crisp, succulent bites at the Big Apple, Harvey had begun, I thought, to weary of it.

Dear John-John:

I am writing you D-Day minus 2 hours, by which I mean it is about to become Xmas eve and the Lord knows what sort of a letter this will turn out to be. But mainly to reassure you: What you failed to do was inconsequential, a subscription entry for Encounter, but long ago I wrote to Master Melvin and he has turned the trick. As a matter of fact, with a vengeance, for I received two copies, a day apart, of the December issue. So you see, I have already turned a profit.

Lowell would be great fun as Oxford professor of Poetry. But don't stick your *own* neck out too far; he has a way of going slightly off his rocker, as you probably know, every now and then. Nothing extreme, but he went that way several weeks ago and his psychiatrist sent him up to his Boston 'home' for recovery. I thought he was behaving queerly a month ago when I ran into him at an off-Broadway play, Cal having Jackie Kennedy at his side, and he was awfully loud, shouting her name at me during introductions. Then Stanley K[unitz] and Nicholas Nabokov both told me he had gone off a bit. And yet how fine he is! Did you see the lovely job he did on nine Mandelstam poems in The N.Y. Review? Most valuable.

Don't worry about your review of the Lowry – let the bits and pieces fall where they may. I have gotten used to obscurity if not failure.

John, should I get out of here? I hate our foreign policy these days, and what has happened in Viet Nam and in Trujilloland gives me nausea. Up until these recent phenomena, I still had an illusion or two about the essential if misguided rightness and goodness of our efforts, but Johnson & Co. have really turned the screw that last turn and I experience a bleakness now as never before. But London? Of course, I'd see you now and then, and a few others, but would I be fearfully lonely? Enforced solitudes are not so pleasant any more. There are the pubs though, and they are essentially friendly.

May! What a lovely month to have a baby. I wish I were there for the christening like the old times. Maybe. Give that beautiful mama my love, and to the family, and to yourself, a great 1966.

Harvey.

One or two other 'matters arising' from the letter. 'Don't worry about your review of the Lowry', refers to a small typographical misadventure. He had edited the letters of Malcolm Lowry, in collaboration with the author's widow Marjorie Bonner Lowry, and I had reviewed the volume in *The New Republic*. Since this magazine was printed in Washington, DC, proof-reading was out of the question, and when I described Harvey's Introduction as having a characteristic blend of enthusiasm and wariness, they printed 'weariness'. I wrote and corrected the slip in the correspondence columns. Next, the references to Robert Lowell. In the last weeks of 1965 it was known that his name was to be put forward as a candidate for the Oxford Chair of poetry, and I supported him, in public and private, all through the campaign until the election in early June 1966 when he in fact came in second to Edmund Blunden. (My misgiving about Blunden as a candidate was that, though a man worthy of great respect, he was too old and tired to do the job, and indeed he had to give it up after struggling for a year to cope with it and rather sadly failing.)

Later in that summer of 1966 Harvey came to London, and once again it was a studio flat and, under the surface liveliness of outings and diversions, a life of the 'awful' loneliness he had feared. He mentioned to me that he was paying court to a girl who was currently the mistress of a well-known actor; eventually, I believe, the actor prevailed, rather as Buck Clayton had prevailed in the case of Mary Lou Williams. Things were going down for Harvey, hopes fading, brightness dimming everywhere.

> The periwinkle and the tough dogfish
> At eventide had got into his dish.

Then came a letter – I have forgotten the year by now, but probably 1967 or 1968 – addressed from some clinic on the West Coast, in which he told me that he had had emergency heart surgery ('it was Marat-Sade') and was now recovering but fitted with a plastic aorta. I sent him the appropriate messages of sympathy, and kept up my correspondence with him, but time was running out. I don't know how long people are supposed to live when the aorta, that massive artery leading from the left ventricle of the heart, is replaced by a plastic tube. Quite a time, I dare say, if it holds, and if nothing else goes. But Harvey never got back onto a winning streak. Not many months passed before one of my letters went unanswered for a long time, and finally there came an answer addressed from the office of some lawyer who was tidying up the details, telling me that Harvey had died.

Werner

THE HILLSIDE lay tilted toward the sea, miles of land facing miles of water. A small road bisected it, not zig-zagging to avoid the steeper parts but ploughing determinedly straight up, like a climber working hard to get to the summit before nightfall. Standing on this steep little road, you were nearly at mid-point of the slope. On either side lay the green, sloping turf, with outcroppings of grey rock, vivid yellow splashes of gorse, here and there a long white single-storied cottage, hugging the ground against the wind from the Irish sea, and the long dark-grey lines of the stone walls. To your left, closing off the view in the distance, stood the line of high, jagged hills called Yr Eifl. English people called these peaks 'the Rivals', not only as being an approximation to the sound of the Welsh name, but because they gave the effect, six or eight of them in a row, of trying to compete and ending up at exactly the same height. If you looked straight ahead you saw the sea, if you looked slightly downwards and towards the right you saw the low-heaped bulk of Anglesey, lying across the mouth of Caernarfon Bay like an enormous stranded whale; and always, from every angle, once you had risen above the treetops and roof-tops of the very lowest part of the hillside, you saw the dark watchful towers of Caernarfon Castle.

These landmarks were immutable. What changed was the light, and with it the colour. They were never the same two days together; hardly, indeed, two hours. Sometimes the land would be dark and the sea bright. The Rivals were always some shade of purple, but the land stretching towards them would often shine with an extraordinarily bright, lyrical green. The flat line of the oceanic horizon would appear sometimes as a thick pencil-stroke of shadow and sometimes as a long ruled line of intense light. Every evening, when the sun sank below that horizon, there was a sunset which I shall not try to describe in words.

The hillside reached its highest point at a long ridge, behind which the ground flattened for a while, as if gathering its breath, and then moved higher in a series of peaks, dominated by Snowdon with its two summits joined by a long scimitar-edge. Dominated, that is, when Snowdon happened to show itself. Very often it retired behind a thick veil of cloud, leaving the other mountains clearly visible, as if being the biggest and most authoritative it had gathered to itself all the available cover and left the others naked. At such times the range, Eryri, viewed from the ridge, looked like a watercolour with Snowdon painted out and grey cloud laid on in its place.

From the road you could not see the mountains. All you could see, if you turned and looked upwards, was the long lip of the ridge and, jutting over it, the long slate-grey ramparts of the quarry, heaped up piece by piece in a century of working. The quarry was silent now. Scattered about its huge level floor, dotted here and there with dark pools that looked unimaginably deep, were pieces of rusting machinery and the occasional hut slowly collapsing in the rain.

The road up the hillside passed through three villages. Each was different in character. The lowest village was set on a gentle slope and the terrain was milder, with trees and bushes. The fields were occupied by calmly chewing cows more often than by nibbling, wind-ruffled sheep. Then the road seemed to shake itself free and push fiercely upwards, as if suddenly impatient of mildness and sociability, and tilted at an angle which made you feel, at times, that you could hardly keep your feet. If you were driving, you went down to second gear on this stretch. It then levelled out, though not much, and passed through the second village, a bleaker and more scattered affair than the first. At the top of this village the road arrived at the ridge, when it turned to the right and went along for a mile or so to the third village, a comfortless place where sheep grazed among the houses as if knowing that the place was just an extension of the bare mountain and the human dwellings had been dumped there by accident. Its chief, or at any rate its largest, building was the big red corrugated-iron shed where the bus rested at night.

Werner lived in the first village, where the air was softer and the trees more numerous, and one smelt the nearness of the sea. His farm was at the end of a long, stony lane. On one side of this lane was a stretch of thistly land with the remains of what looked like a slate railway running along it, the embankment still plain where the metals had gone. On the other, between it and the sharply rising fields, one of those earthworks that are so characteristic of North Wales, hard to describe in a single word since they have some characteristics of a wall and some of a hedge. They result when a stone wall has been standing for generations, its interstices gradually filling up with leaf-mould and bird-droppings and fragments of this and that until there is enough depth for larger plants, such as gorse, to take hold. The accumulation of humus then accelerates until the whole bulwark is hidden beneath vegetation, except here and there where a heavy rainstorm hoses it down and leaves the stones showing through.

These hedge-walls could never be carelessly grubbed up and tossed aside as the farmers in the Midlands have grubbed up and tossed aside their hedges, leaving the land a series of stark, wind-blown prairies. They could only be removed by dynamiting them yard by yard. They give us a clue to the temperament of the North Welsh people.

To get to Werner's farm you had to open a metal gate which bore in neat writing the name 'Hafodty Wernlas'. The slight similarity of the second part of the name to Werner's own name was nothing to do with his living there; it was simply a coincidence. Closing the gate behind you – for Werner usually had a few cows thriftily chewing up what sustenance they could find on the stretch of land where the old railway had run – you went on for two or three hundred yards and there, inside another of those standard metal five-barred gates, was the farm with its low-roofed outbuildings and byres and its sheltered garden from which, looking over the treetops, you could make out the sea at no great distance.

Werner would usually be standing in the farmyard, or moving about in one of the nearby fields. (His farm was not large
enough for the fields to be anything but nearby.) In such an
intensely Welsh setting, he struck one at once as conspicuously
foreign: a big, burly German with a bony face, his deep-set eyes
looking out from under the duck-billed cap that by itself
made him seem foreign when he stood among the local farmers
with their universal flat tweed caps. 'Grüss Gott, Werner,' I
would say, and he would reply 'Grüss Gott, John.' I do not in
fact speak German and was not trying to come on as an expert in
things Teutonic. But there seemed no other natural way to
greet him. A tame English 'hello' seemed, under the circumstances, ridiculous, and though after decades in that countryside he spoke Welsh well enough, I didn't.

Werner was a country boy from somewhere in what is now
called East Germany. When Hitler came to power, Werner was
a boy of eleven or twelve in a poor working-class household.
When Hitler decided that the time was ripe for the *Herrenvolk*
to impose their will on the rest of the world by military might,
he put the German young men into uniform and armed them.
Werner was put into the uniform, and given the weapons,
of the Afrika Corps. He went to North Africa; he fought in the
desert; he was captured by, I suppose, the soldiers of the Eighth
Army.

Then followed a passage in Werner's life which, though he
explained it to me once or twice, I have never been quite clear
about. Perhaps his explanations were themselves not quite
clear. Perhaps the young soldier, pitched into one alien environment and then another and then another, was a little dazed
about what was happening to him. When he recounted his
memories, the pictures would blur into one another. He and his
Afrika Corps comrades were on a crowded troop-train, going
down through Italy to whatever port it was from which they
were going to sail to North Africa, stopping briefly at Italian
stations, getting off to buy wine and sausages and bread and

hurrying back on to the train, Werner being proud of the astuteness with which he avoided being swindled by the Italian pedlars . . . Some of his comrades were swindled, but not Werner because he knew what to look out for and what things ought to cost . . . Werner in a prison camp in Minnesota, where no one ever tried to escape because they could hear the wolves howling outside the fence in the freezing nights . . . Werner, still wearing P.O.W. uniform, working on a farm outside Caernarfon . . . Exactly by what stages he had got from the North African desert to the icy lake-dotted plains of Minnesota and thence to the coast of North Wales he never explained coherently, and perhaps the whole kaleidoscope was never coherent in his own mind. But it was all quite simple really: give the kaleidoscope a quick shake, the images jump into a new pattern, and there is Werner, still young, but out of uniform now, working as a farm manager somewhere along the green rocky coast of Gwynedd.

He was also, at the same time, planning a voyage along the rocky coast of matrimony. There is, or was in those days, a chain of cafés in those seaside towns, called Harper's; pleasant, clean, moderate in prices; old-fashioned, in a reassuring way, places of the tea-and-scones rather than the hamburger-and-coke variety. Werner used to take his tea and scones in the Harper's Café that looked across the Castle Square at Caernarfon. The brisk, capable young manageress came to recognise him, looked on him with favour, shared with him the delicious pangs of mutual attraction, and one more marriage went down in the statistics.

I don't know the early stages of Werner's domestic life; by the time I met him, in about 1961, he was well settled with his wife and daughter in Hafodty Wernlas, rooted in the local community. They knew him, of course, as 'the German', and never got round to using his surname. That never surprised me, for in that district all of us who were not Welsh were inevitably lumped together as foreigners. A man who lived in a house beside the mountain road, and who had been settled there for years for the benefit of his health, was always known as 'the Englishman'. That was enough to differentiate him; six hundred years of (nominal) political unification with England cut no ice with these hill Welsh.

During all those summers, our sons ran about the hillside, discovering the world, companionable with birds and animals, smelling the gorse and heather and the sea wind; and, in most weathers, barefoot from April to October, so that today, as grown men, they have perfect feet. Our cottage was directly above Werner's farm – on the next shelf, so to speak. If we walked two or three hundred yards into the wild country that lay over our wall, we could look down on his long low roof.

Though nothing would have made him say so directly, I always had the impression that Werner envied us our three healthy sons. I know he would have liked to sire a line of farmers, and I think it struck me as an example of the injustice of the universe that he, the big strong farmer, had to be content with having sired an only daughter while I, the writer, half his size, half his weight and not a third of his strength, had three resplendent sons.

Not, I hasten to say, that Werner was anything but deeply fond of his daughter. She tended, like many a girl with a big, slow, patient father, to order him about, but he did not seem to mind much. One instance of her ordering him about put him into a situation of some difficulty, but also enabled him to show German practicality and thoroughness, so perhaps it was not wasted.

It happened one evening when, after the usual hard day, Werner had his boots off by the fire, and a glass or two inside him. The telephone rang: his daughter, out with some friends in Bangor or somewhere equally remote, had missed the impossibly early last bus home. He was to turn out and drive over to fetch her.

Werner pulled himself away from the fire, arrayed himself and drove off to pick her up. On the way he was stopped by a police patrol, breathalysed, and subsequently convicted of driving with those fatal few glasses inside him. Twelve months' disqualification.

During those twelve months, Werner coped manfully enough. He used the bus, he used the telephone, he had other people drive him. Only one problem bulked large: his lunch-time beer in the pub at the bottom of the hill. After a long morning's work, he needed it, and he could not lay in elaborate supplies at home because his wife was strict about his drinking.

Ingenuity triumphed. Leaning about in various parts of the farm, Werner had three bicycles. So big and heavy a man was not a natural cyclist, but he could pedal as far as the end of his lane, and once he had done that he was on the road that swooped down the hill. All he had to do was balance, and ring his bell, and hunch down against the wind like a T.T. rider, and he was at the pub. There, he propped his bicycle against the wall, went in, had his fill of beer and conversation, and could always rely on someone giving him a lift back up the hill as the session drew to its end. Repeat with bicycles no.2 and no.3. On day 4, he went down with his tractor and trailer (no policeman would dream of stopping a farmer with a tractor in the middle of the day), loaded up the bicycles, and started the process again.

That was the Werner I knew in his prime, his heyday when the sun of his life was at high noon and throwing strong vertical shadows. Small misfortunes were jokes, to be countered by measures that were in themselves counter-jokes, and at that time of his life I do not think he had much in the way of larger misfortunes. I remember him as burly, confident, filling a room, always slightly larger than life-size. And always tremendously, overwhelmingly *German*. German in his genial, open-handed hospitality, German in his long, slow descents into melancholy. When he appeared in the pub, everyone had to drink up and take charge of a fresh, brimming glass – *had* to, since any attempt to say that one was just going, didn't want any more, was late for the next appointment, simply fell on deaf ears. He didn't hear it and so you hadn't said it. I have never lost my driving licence through drinking too much, but if I had it would certainly have been Werner's fault. How often he has borne down on me, his huge hand gripped round a pint glass, and swept me into the vortex of his hospitality. And then there were the times when he would become muted, sentimental, almost lachrymose. A few bars from Beethoven, heard by chance on the radio, would be enough to plunge him into a Werther-like trance of sensibility. At such times he would come out with his deeper thoughts on politics, society, history, and the glimpses thus afforded were not always reassuring.

'John,' he said to me once, confidingly, in one of these reflective spells, 'isn't it a pity Hitler went mad?' He meant, of course, that it was a pity Hitler had caused Germany to lose the war, and in that moment I saw clearly the whole reason why Hitler had been able to muster behind his crackpot theories and hysterical play-acting the vast concentrated strength of the German people. Werner, a perfect example of the men who had suffered the consequences of Hitler's policies in their own lives, was ready to have forgiven Hitler everything if he had not 'gone mad', i.e., had succeeded in his aims. I tried to indicate, briefly and emphatically, that Hitler's policies and his world-view had been sick, evil, twisted, from the moment he first appeared on the public stage. But Werner was unshakeable. From his angle, Hitler had started out as the champion and deliverer of the German people, however things had gone wrong later. 'My fader had no job. Then comes Hitler. Then my fader had a job.' Obviously all the sick, neurotic side of Hitler's theories – the vindictive search for a racial scapegoat, the systematic exploitation of grievances, the hysterical cult of male potency, the shibboleth of racial purity – had gone over his head completely unnoticed – either that, or they had fitted so smoothly in with some kind of interior pattern, some inner core of German-ness, that – once again – he had simply not noticed them.

Yes, there were sides to Werner that one feared and distrusted: not in terms of the man himself, but in terms of what they would mean if they were bloated out, multiplied by hundreds of thousands, put into uniform and set marching with the power of a great and restless nation behind them. As himself, as the individual Werner from Hafodty Wernlas, staring out at life under that long-peaked cap, he was nothing but likeable and trustworthy: and this has always been the German paradox.

I could not help liking Werner, not that I ever made the slightest effort to do anything *but* like him. So many features of his personality, and his way of life, struck chords in me, deep ancestral chords. His small, mixed farm was a home to me before I ever saw it or knew of its existence. Like many people who come from a background where no one owned anything much, so that there are no heirlooms and very few documents, I know little about my ancestry, and cannot even trace it back further than about a century. What I do know for certain is that my parentage straddles two adjacent counties. My father's people were workers in the pottery industry in North Staffordshire, and my mother's were smallholders in Cheshire, in the area round about Middlewich and Nantwich (what solid, uncompromising Anglo-Saxon names!). English agriculture has tended to be an affair of masters and employees, but the peasant, the farmer who owns a small amount of land and farms it without employed labour, the more easily if he is blessed with strong sons, is a type that has existed here and there in England, and my mother's family belonged to it; her own mother had been born and bred on a farm in South Cheshire. I have, then, peasant blood in my veins to the extent of one-eighth of the total, and when I stood with Werner in his ancient, low-raftered byre or wandered around his pig-styes and cabbage-patch and trod his two or three sloping fields, I was breathing an air that had gone towards my own making.

Keeping company with Werner was also a way in which I could pass on this thread to my own offspring. One afternoon, I walked down to his farm at about five o'clock with the three boys, William, Ianto and Toby, aged at that time about fifteen, thirteen and nine. Werner was not about in the farmyard. We

found him in the cowshed, assisting at the birth of a calf. I don't
know how long the labour had been going on when we arrived;
it had reached the stage when the calf had one leg out into the
open (was this the equivalent, I wondered, of a 'breech birth'?),
and round this leg Werner had tied a length of rope. As
we came blinking in from the bright sunlight into the cool shade
of the byre, he immediately conscripted us as a labour force.
The boys were set to pull, exactly like a tug-of-war team, on the
rope attached to the calf's leg. Leaning steeply, they pulled with
all their might; the cow laboured; and Werner, gentle and
compassionate, sat with her head in his lap, stroking her head
and patting her neck, saying over and over, 'Good girl, there's a
good girl, oh, she's a good girl, a good girl.' At last the birth was
accomplished. A sleek wet new animal landed on the concrete
floor, to be gathered up immediately by Ianto. Some years later
I read a poem by Ted Hughes in which a newborn calf is
described as 'wet as a collie from the river,' and the words
brought back that sleek, soaking creature, held so protectively
in Ianto's arms. I felt sure then, and I feel sure now, that my
sons would from that moment on have a more understanding
and a more tender eye for birth and indeed for life itself.

Such things, in abundance, I and mine owed to my friendship with Werner. Could he be said to owe anything to his
friendship with me?

Much less, inevitably. I was a marginal figure in his life. Still,
I had my place. For one thing, I was one of the few people with
whom he came into regular contact who had any mental picture
of that European land-mass where he had his roots and from
which he derived so much of his being. I do not know Germany, having been there only the once and not speaking the
language, but I had some acquaintance, partly imaginative and
partly through direct experience, of rural places in Europe
where his counterparts were to be found. One winter, drinking
a glass of white wine in a roadside café at a pinpoint village in the
Alpes Vaudoises called La Comballaz, I found myself looking
across the room at a knot of peasant farmers sitting round a

table, drinking a carafe and settling some matter of business. Their hard, bony bodies, their weather-beaten, concentrated faces looking out attentively from beneath the brims of battered hats, all seemed familiar to me, and I realised that – *mutatis mutandis* – I was looking at so many Werners. That same day I sent him a post-card: greetings from one mountain world to another.

As a frequent drinking companion, I was also welcome in his life as a confidant. Werner liked a drink. His liking for a drink was not, in its turn, liked in his household. He and his wife let off part of their house to holiday visitors every summer, and this source of income involved Werner's wife, as well as Werner himself, in a great deal of extra work. Obviously she could not stand for a husband who breathed alcoholic fumes over the guests and even, on occasion, showed up slightly glassy-eyed. A foot was put down. Werner became adept at taking a drink on the sly. Once, when I was having a conversation with him in the cowshed, he reached up a hand and brought down a half-full bottle of gin which had been standing on one of the ancient beams above our heads. Taking off the cap, he took a generous swig and offered the bottle to me. Finding neat gin totally nauseating, I had no difficulty in refusing.

We spent a good part of every summer in our cottage on the hillside, and sometimes Easter and a spell in the autumn too, and one year we made a visit, memorable alike for beauty and austerity, in midwinter. The rich tangle of the hillside, the intoxicating scent made up of heather, gorse and the breath of the sea, the immense view spread out in front, entered into the characters of our growing sons as they had long ago entered ours. And always, Werner was part of it.

I have always had a great deal of sympathy with the ancient belief in the *genius loci*, the notion that not only every individual human soul, but every place, had a tutelary spirit. Werner inhabited the hillside so naturally that he seemed like the presiding spirit of the place. The hardness of the rocks was in his bony face, his thinning hair was like the sparse, fine mountain grass, in his size and strength he trod the pasture like a quiet bull. And just as nature is ceaselessly at work, so was he. His few fields were cared for and cropped with tireless attention. When he was not doing the farm work, he was building: mixing concrete, laying bricks, wheeling stone and timber back and forth. He built on to his farmhouse extra accommodation for the summer visitors, and took his share in the chores involved. At about five in the afternoon, a common time for me to walk down to see him, I usually found him in an outhouse sitting in front of an enormous mound of vegetables which he was peeling and scraping and cutting up for the evening meal.

Intensely German in his unlimited capacity for work and his compensating fondness for deep draughts at the pub, Werner also reflected his German origins (and, no doubt, the Central European peasant tradition in general) in being a shrewd and thrifty man of business. He kept a watchful eye on property that fell vacant in the surrounding villages, and every now and then he would snap one up and with his knowledge of all sides of the building trade he would set to work carpentering, retiling, making concrete paths, strengthening walls, finding the spare hours from somewhere and doing most of the work himself, till he had a spruce, weathertight building, one more investment.

Perhaps it could be said, looking at the matter from a certain point of view, that this thrift and forethought helped in the end to undermine the foundations of Werner's domestic life. One year, when I met him soon after I arrived on the hillside (we did not keep up during the winter and always had to begin by hearing one another's news), he greeted me with, 'John, mine vife has left me.' It is true that he immediately flashed a self-mocking grin, as if he had merely been joking, and never alluded directly to the matter again. But it was, as I soon discovered, the case that his wife had moved into one of the other houses they owned, down at sea-level and more convenient for town, and that she had taken a job in Caernarfon. The only times after that when Werner referred to the matter were simply rather insistent references to how he saw his wife often, how he had his regular evenings for visiting her, how they played gramophone records together. But the fact remained that he was alone in the farmhouse. The summer visitors shrank from a regular all-season full house to a few old habitués, often single men, who had their settled habits and looked after themselves. If I dropped in to see him in the evenings I would find him sitting in the kitchen by himself.

And now, other changes began to come over him. His German accent, which had always been conspicuous, now seemed to gather strength. There were times when he handled English almost as slowly and cumbrously as he must have done when he was first shipped over from that Minnesota camp with the wolves howling outside. He became more sententious, as if he were trying to gather up the lessons of his life and hand them on to posterity, and in these moods he would refer to himself in the third person, as if describing some proverbial figure. 'Now listen, boys,' he would say to my sons, 'I'm going to tell you sommsing. Werner is clever.' At the words 'Werner is clever' he would tap his great lined dome with a solemn forefinger.

His talk, now, turned increasingly on the past, on his boyhood and his days in the army. I used to spend evenings with him, over a bottle of white wine, in which he would shuffle press-cuttings about and try to piece his story together, as if it was important, now, to review it all in memory and get it into some order. He was pleased when a young woman who worked on a local paper sought him out and interviewed him about his experiences. There was even some talk, he told me proudly, of her visiting him over a period of time and assembling enough material for a series of articles or even a book. With idle facetiousness I suggested that with the fair reporter coming to visit him often in his lonely farmhouse, he might be in line for a beautiful emotional experience. Immediately his expression became grave: 'Ach, no, John, I love mine vife.'

I was genuinely interested in Werner's memories and encouraged him to talk them out. Others found him less sympathetic; and these, to be fair, were not summer visitors but his regular,

all-the-year-round neighbours who had to cope with him on a
daily level. He began to stay longer in the pub and drink more
heavily; of the two public houses that were anywhere near his
home, he became unpopular at one and was no longer welcomed. The customers at the other were shocked to find him
one night, after they thought he had gone home, lying on the
pavement a few yards from the door. That was as much of the
journey home as he could manage.

At the end of the 1970s, my life entered a period of upheaval
and change. Everyone's life is changing all the time, of course,
but still there are some periods that stand out as cataclysms.
The details don't matter; though this book has, obviously, its
biographical element, it is not *un journal intime*. I doubt if I
shall ever write *un journal intime*, and if I do it will take a very
different form from the present book; it will probably be in
verse, for one thing. Thinking back to Werner, however, one
point that has to be made is that the pressures and dislocations
reached a pitch at which Eirian and I moved apart and did not
live together for three and a half years.

When the storm cleared and the sun came out again, many
things in the landscape had changed, naturally. Our boys had
become grown men, for one thing, and left the nest; one of
them now makes his home in the cottage on the hillside. But the
particular quality of my memories of Werner is that they are
pre-storm memories. At the stage when I thought the break
between us was going to be permanent, I knew I had in future to
keep clear of the cottage and its environment; it is Eirian's
house and the setting is ancestral to her and not to me; my rights
there had (as I thought) expired.

1982 was the first year in which I did not go up. It would have
been Year Twenty-Three. When it came to that point in the
summer when Werner had been accustomed to our arriving
in the neighbourhood, when he would have begun to look
out for me walking in the steep fields or sitting in the bar
parlour, I wondered what he would think, and how he
would react to being told that our casual meetings, our

long-established small rituals, would not come again.

As it happened, he never did know. At just about the time when he would normally have begun expecting to see me, early July, he took to his bed and died. To me his death came as a deep and piercing shock. Foolish though I know it to be, I have never been able to root out from my mind the thought that I killed him.

Summer, and Shakespeare,
and a Welsh Cadet

ON A SULTRY August morning in 1984, I was drinking my usual cup of tea and listening to the 8 a.m. radio; and it informed me, along with the other news, that Richard Burton had died during the night. I was sorry to hear it, for he was only fifty-eight and might reasonably have hoped for a good spell of life yet; but I did not expect that his death would affect me very nearly, that it would get right in among my emotions and stir up deep-layered memories. I had liked Burton, and in many ways admired his power as an actor, and certainly I had been glad of his success. But I knew that my part in his life, and his in mine, were buried many years down; forty years, to be precise, since we had performed together, and been good friends and seen a lot of each other, in the summer of 1944.

Since then, we had met just once, having a very pleasant lunch together when he and Elizabeth Taylor were staying at the Bear Hotel in Woodstock and I drove over to spend a couple of hours with them, eating, drinking and reminiscing. But I had no particular reason to think that I would see him again. We were aware of each other and wished each other well, but our lives were enormously far apart. In short, he figured in my mind as a person I had once known; his face and words and gestures belonged to a specific moment in my growing-up, and he could hardly have been less of a presence in my life if he had already been dead for years.

I didn't, then, expect the news of his death to affect me much. And yet it did affect me. Not with a sense of grief or loss, exactly; it was more a sense of finality. Certain memories became fixed, like photographs that are developed; by dying, he had closed a book on a few of whose pages my youthful figure could be seen making its exits and entrances.

Burton and I were undergraduate contemporaries; not at the same College, but in the shrunken war-time University the barriers of College were of even less account than they are normally. I had presented myself for my medical the year before and been turned down, having bad eyesight already at that age. This left me with nothing to do but finish my time out at Oxford, so that my undergraduate dates are 1943-6. Richard for his part was 'a cadet'. This term will require explanation. The Armed Services, thinking that they would benefit by a certain intake of the kind of men the University produced, instituted a scheme whereby men already enlisted came up to College and spent six months, partly on academic work and partly on military training. The University, on its side, undertook to have these men back, if they survived the war, to read a formal degree: a promise that was honoured.

Cadets took their six months either in the form of October to March, or April to September, according to when they arrived. If it was the latter, they had a special term laid on during the three-month Long Vacation. Richard Burton and I were both in Oxford in August, 1944 – the deadest point of the Long Vac – he because he was having his cadet term, I because I was taking advantage of the war-time regulation that you could live in College free of charge as long as you 'fire-watched', i.e. stayed up certain hours of the night, in a rota, to be ready to extinguish the blaze from air raids that, mercifully, never came.

So, as I cycled into town on the thundery evening of that same day, I contemplated the alleys and entries and pub doorways that I had first explored in his company forty Augusts before: contemplated them with an intensity quickened by that sense of finality, the closing of those pages.

It was not only the chances of war that had brought us together. Shakespeare, as so often, was at work in the background somewhere. His influence on my life has been incalculable. One of the reasons why Richard Burton's death struck in my mind that plangent little note of finality was because it reduced by one, and an important one, the number of those who had experienced at first hand the magic of performing Shakespeare under the guidance of Nevill Coghill. In writing of Coghill I mentioned the strong central thread of his effort, across twenty years, to gain acceptance for his ideas and perceptions about Shakespeare by means of an annual summer production at Oxford, and how this effort had if anything earned him disapproval. That disapproval has long since been forgotten, of course, and yet I am convinced that the greatness of Coghill as an illuminator of Shakespeare is not yet recognised. These productions, after all, were evanescent; they were spoken into summer air by performers who were not, for the most part, going on to be professionally concerned with the theatre or with literature; they could not be written down and printed, like lectures, nor did they remain fixed for ever like films. And, since Nevill's medium of work was the production, the demonstration in action of how he understood a play, he did not really do himself justice when in later years he came to write his one full-length book on the subject, *Shakespeare's Professional Skills*.

When Nevill produced a play he started with a radiant vision of what the play was conveying. (I avoid saying 'its meaning', since if a play had a 'meaning' that could be printed out, we could all just take the print-out and there would be no need for a production.) It was not his way to assemble the cast and lecture them on his interpretation of the play before beginning to rehearse; quite apart from anything else, to present a cut-and-dried view at the outset would have been to assume in advance that he was not going to learn anything during the course of production. He allowed his view to permeate the minds of his actors, in asides, in the more or less idle chat during moments of relaxation or as one strolled back to College after a rehearsal. And it was all inseparable, for us young, impressionable people, from what is nowadays called Nevill's 'charisma', his personal influence, that presence, large, strong, friendly and still authoritative. Nevill obviously drew so much life and strength from Shakespeare that it seemed impossible that each of us, in our different ways, would not draw life and strength from him too.

Nevill's interpretations were in line with his general attitude, as of course they would have to be. He was a Christian; not the intellectual, theological kind like C.S. Lewis, but a Christian influenced by Jung, seeing the symbolic power of the Christian diagram repeated in all great European art. (There is a superb passage towards the end of his brilliant short book *The Poet Chaucer* in which he comes closest to expounding his central view of high 'comedy', using the word as Dante used it in the title of his great poem.) As a critic of Shakespeare, he worked always from the inside of the play, getting to its heart and, so to speak, switching on lights that then shone outwards, rather than training a fierce light on the play's exterior shell and hoping by that means to penetrate to its heart.

Richard Burton and I had taken part in Nevill's production of *Measure for Measure* in June 1944. At that late and critical point in the war (and it wasn't lost on me that while I was acting Shakespeare, others of my generation were fighting desperate battles on Normandy beaches – but then, how *does* a non-combatant keep the flag flying? What *ought* he to do?) – at that point, I say, every kind of material was very scarce, paper particularly so, and the programme for *Measure for Measure* was no exception; a single sheet of thickish paper, with a design on one side and a cast list and various credits on the other, it (to use the time-hallowed phrase) 'lies before me as I write'. The Recto side is given over to a design, photographically reproduced from pencil; it was executed, I remember, by a young man at the Slade School of Art, housed in Oxford during the war. The keynote is speculation, a producer's jottings, the sort of drawing that one does on a blotting-pad while thinking out some important problem. In the centre is a composite drawing of a face, or rather several faces blended into one: a bearded full-face bisected by two, then three, faces gazing into each other's eyes, the expressions gentle and accepting. Down one side are pencilled notes like the jottings from a working rehearsal. The young art student has very effectively taken Nevill's instructions and made the design into the clip-board of a deeply absorbed, creative director.

as you from crimes
      would pardoned be
  let your indulgence set me free

(play of forgiveness)
  more than the tempest

isabel forgives in the
  moment of direst loss.

thus hath pieres
      power be his
  pardon payed
      to bynde to unbynde

And, longitudinally up the side: 'judge not that ye be not judged for with what measure ye mete it shall be meted to you again.'

There was no space for a programme note, but in those few cryptic jottings all Nevill's preoccupations are plain; *Piers Plowman*; the theme of Christian forgiveness in Shakespeare; the fact that *Measure for Measure* is the only one of Shakespeare's plays with a title from the Gospels.

Nevill did not do the 1945 production; the programme for his next venture, *A Winter's Tale* in 1946, is also looking up at me as I write. The two years that have gone by have made a little more paper sparingly available, and this programme does at least run to a folded sheet, giving four sides for printing on. The outside sheet (Recto 1) has a black-and-white drawing, crude enough, a mere sketch but powerful and suggestive, showing a stylized crowned figure with eyes downcast. One half of the face is in darkness, or perhaps it is a skull; the other in light; the crown is inscribed TIME, and radiating out from the figure are six semi-circles on either side. The series on our left (the figure's right) is embellished with a dark sword, that on the other side with what looks like a stylized olive branch or garland of peace of some sort. The circles contain the words, moving inwards to the centre: *Right*; MALE/ TRAGEDY: DIVINE WRATH/ CAMILLO/ FLORIZEL/ POLIXENES/ MAMILLIUS; *Left*: FEMALE/

COMEDY: FESTIVAL/ PAULINA/ PERDITA/ HERMIONE/ LEONTES. It will be seen that this is not immediately self-explanatory; we want to know, for instance, why the name LEONTES should appear on the female side, and in its innermost ring at that. But Nevill's explanations of things were always voyages of discovery, rather than cut-and-dried patterns where everything was assigned to its comprehended place. Nevill's programme note shows his usual fertility of suggestion and depth of involvement:

This strange and exciting play, sharply split by a great gap in Time into Tragedy and Comedy, Death and Rebirth, does not seem a study of any actual world, such as was the Roman world of *Antony and Cleopatra*, but of a semi-fabulous or Dream-world, where life has the shape of parable.

For no reason, The Ancient Mariner shot the Albatross, and passed through an expiation that can never end, for Coleridge saw in guilt a self-inflicted wound that cannot quite heal over; The Mariner has to tell his tale on and on and for ever.

Equally for no reason, Leontes yields to a sudden, foul and false suspicion, bringing death to his son and seeming death to his wife and child, death to all hope of new generation, seeming death to his soul; and in doing this he drives out another part of himself; he splits friendship away in Polixenes. But in Shakespeare guilt is not inexpiable; the self-inflicted wound can heal; Conscience, in Paulina, teaches him a long but fruitful penitence, which, under the hand of Time and of the Gods, is acceptable to them; the Oracle is fulfilled. Young hope grows and returns, linking Leontes with the love and friendship he had forfeited, and in that festival, Hermione, who seems a symbol for his soul, under the care of Conscience, comes back to life with music, like Eurydice; unlike Eurydice, not to be snatched away, but to walk with him alive out of the healing dream, with all that had been split away joined and made whole and happy.

It seems to me that that brief note contains enough ideas about *A Winter's Tale* to be expanded, if one had the leisure, into a whole book, yet it is a solidly cohesive, self-consistent approach, not a coruscation of assorted ideas such as the brain-teeming Marshall would have offered.

Each of Nevill's productions was illuminated by a major central idea, but because the idea was embodied in speech and gesture and facial expression and movement, it remained a part of the play and could not be, or at any rate resisted being, taken out and brandished as a detachable entity. It amazes me, looking back, that his work in these productions should have been not only unappreciated but, in some University circles, actually counted against him. I believe all of us who took part in them were enriched and helped. We came away with a better grip on Shakespeare and a deeper love for his work. Certainly that was true of two adolescents who acted for him in 1944, when we put on *Measure for Measure* in the tiny cloistered quadrangle at the back entrance of the Cathedral at Christ Church, using the great stone steps, as well as the space at their foot, as an acting area. Burton played the part of Angelo, I of Claudio. As a glance at the text will confirm. Claudio and Angelo have no scene together, so I can't, strictly speaking, claim to have 'acted with' Richard Burton in the sense of having exchanged dialogue with him on stage. But I watched and listened as he mastered his part, and his way of uttering some of the speeches is as fresh in my mind today as it was then: particularly the speech in II, ii, when Angelo's self-righteousness has first been pierced by sudden longing for physical possession of the chaste Isabella:

> What's this? What's this? Is this her fault or mine?
> The tempter or the tempted, who sins most?

and onward for twenty electrifying lines. His voice was already

powerful and resonant, his stage presence confident. The rest
of us held him in some awe because, where we had mostly
arrived at the University straight from school, Burton had
actually 'been on the stage'; he had toured with a little fit-up
repertory company, and that was glamour in our eyes. Of
course we recognised him as a better actor than the rest of us,
though the enormous difference between us did not open out
till later.

Those crowded weeks in June – somehow not diminished but
rather sharpened and heightened by the knowledge that others,
including many of our own contemporaries, were having an
even more crowded time, fighting desperate battles in Normandy – gave us a richness of shared experience that compensated
for the shortness of the time we had known each other. When I
came back to Oxford in August, to stay there for the rest of the
Long Vacation, I looked him up and we at once fell into a
routine of spending our evenings together, sometimes *à deux*
but more often with a man named Conway, a friend of Burton's
from the same College, Exeter.

Conway was, I think, a West Country lad, large, humorous,
easy-going. He was the perfect companion on our evening
rambles. In particular, he had an enormous repertoire of
Victorian and Edwardian music-hall songs. He knew the words
of such immortal ditties as 'Any Old Iron' and 'One of The
Ruins that Cromwell Knocked Abaht a Bit' – not merely the
choruses, which most of us knew, but the connecting verses
that introduced them. For instance:

Just a week or two ago me pore old Uncle Bill
Went an' kicked the bucket an' 'e lef' me in 'is will:
The other day I popped arahnd to see me Auntie Jane,
She sez 'Your Uncle Bill 'as left to you (*slow*) a watch an' chain . . .

I put it on – right across me chess –
Thought I looked a dandy as it dangled from me vess:
Jes' to flash it off I started walkin' rahnd abaht,
A lot of kiddies follered me (*slow*) and they began to shaht . . .

(*Chorus*)   Any old iron, any old iron,
                  Any any any old iron, etc.

Burton and I eagerly soaked up these refrains from Conway and the three of us used to sing them as we walked around the airless streets from one pub to another.

I am not going to pretend that Burton, Conway and I did anything particularly remarkable during those leisure hours we spent together. We went to pubs; Burton taught me to play bar billiards, and I believe I have thought of him, however fleetingly, during every game of bar billiards I have had since. For the rest, he talked, and I listened. He had much more to talk about than I had: quite apart from having been 'on the stage', he had a whole differentiated culture to which with a great part of his being he belonged, that of Wales, and he took pleasure in bringing it before our eyes. He talked about rugby matches, with the passionate, cheering, singing crowds, and the players who would often be men who had spent the morning working a shift at the coal-face. He spoke of the furious pace of these games, of how he had seen a man killed by running head-first against a goal-post when swerving to avoid the tackle that would have stopped him scoring a try. He talked of preachers and their hold on the emotions of the crowded chapel congregations. 'There was one, he'd look round the chapel before he started, and pick on the woman he thought would be easiest to make cry. Then when he started to preach, he'd pitch it all at this woman, keeping on and on at her till she started crying, and then of course it spread and they were all crying.' Most of his stories were about the grotesque, disproportionate side of Welsh life, but his love of that life was obvious. I did not know at that time how important Wales was to be in my own life, how I was destined to have a Welsh wife and three half-Welsh sons, how it was to become very much a second country to me, but Burton fired my imagination. I already knew it as a beautiful country, I had seen the mountains, but up to then I had experienced it as a landscape without people. Later that same summer I began to read the poems of Dylan Thomas, not at Burton's recommendation (he never mentioned Thomas and I don't believe at that time he had heard of him) but merely as part of a general curiosity about contemporary poetry; and the discovery of the lilt and intensity of Thomas's verse has fused in my mind with those evenings spent listening to Richard Burton; so that the association, ten years later, of Burton the actor with Thomas the playwright, in that posthumous production of *Under Milk Wood*, seemed to me a thing as natural as the rain falling on the trees.

Burton was (what I took to be) typically Welsh in his love of language and especially his deep delight in the spoken word. When he had taken a few drinks, he broke into recitation as naturally as some people, in like circumstances, break into song. One night we were at a party; I have totally forgotten who gave this party, or who was there, except that it was somewhere in Ship Street. Burton, who had been rather quiet (he was not, in company, a noisy man, not one of those explosive talkers who think of themselves as the 'life and soul' of a gathering), suddenly stood up, went over to the bookcase, and took out a Bible. Turning rapidly to II Samuel 18, he read out the account of the death of Absalom and the lamentation of David.

> And behold, Cushi came; and Cushi said, Tidings, my lord the king: for the Lord hath avenged thee this day of all them that rose up against thee. And the king said unto Cushi, Is the young man Absalom safe? And Cushi answered, The enemies of my lord the king, and all that rise against thee to do thee hurt, be as that young man is. And the king was much moved, and went up to the chamber over the gate, and wept: and as he went, thus he said, O my son Absalom, my son, my son Absalom! would God I had died for thee, O Absalom, my son, my son!

Then he slipped the book back on to the shelf and himself

slipped back into the rhythm of the party. But I remember the voice, the eyes, the magnetic stillness of his body as he spoke.

Richard helped me, a little, towards growing up. At nineteen, I was still very close to what I had been like as a schoolboy, whereas he was a young adult. His attitude to life was more independent, less anxiety-ridden, than mine. We talked often, inevitably, of 'sex', and I remember bringing up what was to me then the burning question, What did one Use? (To me and most of the youths in my circle, the ultimate nightmare was the thought of getting a girl with child; in those days it nearly always led to a shotgun marriage, which could involve years, if not a lifetime, of misery.) Burton gave me a humorous shrug and said, 'I never use anything.' I wondered how he had got away with it. (I am still wondering how he got away with it, as a matter of fact.)

I remember other small instances of his freer, less dauntable attitude. To play bar billiards you put sixpence into a slot in the table, which released the requisite balls until, after a set time, they began to drop down a row of inviolable *oubliettes*. One evening we had just inserted our sixpence when the landlord called Time. He began moving around the bar, collecting up glasses and generally speeding departure, when our game had hardly got under way, and came and stood beside us insisting that it was time to leave. I, after years of a savage discipline at school, was timid of anyone in authority, and would probably have slunk out leaving the game half-finished, but Burton imperturbably refused to move. 'We've got to get our tanner's worth, old man,' he said reasonably to the landlord.

On that day some twenty years later when I had lunch with the Burtons in their hotel at Woodstock, I asked Richard if he knew what had happened to Conway. He told me Conway had stayed on in the Air Force as a regular officer and had spent his time flying the most advanced fighter aircraft. 'Drunk from morning to night,' he added. I am sure the last sentence was mere embroidery, based on our memories of Conway's convivial habits: no one could fly those fierce contraptions who was not cold sober and completely alert. But I was glad to have word of our friend.

That, as I say, was two decades after our summer together, and now as I write this another two decades have passed. I don't know where Conway is; and for that matter I don't know where Burton is. But I am here, remembering them.